		DATE DUE		

SMART MONEY
The Story of Bill Gates

SMART MONEY
The Story of Bill Gates

Aaron Boyd

MORGAN REYNOLDS *Publishing, Inc.*

620 South Elm Street, Suite 223
Greensboro, North Carolina 27406
http://www.morganreynolds.com

SMART MONEY: THE STORY OF BILL GATES

Copyright © 2004 by Aaron Boyd

Library of Congress Cataloging-in-Publication Data

Boyd, Aaron, 1955-
  Smart money : the story of Bill Gates / Aaron Boyd.— Rev. ed.
    p. cm. — (American business leaders)
Originally published in series: Notable Americans.
Includes bibliographical references and index.
  ISBN 1-931798-32-X (library binding)
  1. Gates, Bill, 1955—Juvenile literature. 2. Businesspeople—United
States—Biography—Juvenile literature. 3. Computer software
industry—United States—Juvenile literature. [1. Gates, Bill, 1955- 2.
Businesspeople. 3. Computer software industry. 4. Microsoft
Corporation—History.] I. Title. II. Series.
  HD9696.C62B69 2004
  338.7'610053'092—dc22

                                     2003024616

Printed in the United States of America
Revised Edition

To Joseph

Contents

Chapter One
Trey 9

Chapter Two
Lakeside 17

Chapter Three
Teenage Programmer 26

Chapter Four
Harvard 34

Chapter Five
BASIC Beginnings 39

Chapter Six
Microsoft 48

Chapter Seven
DOS 55

Chapter Eight
Interface War 65

Chapter Nine
Windows 75

Chapter Ten
Competition 84

Chapter Eleven
Microsoft at War 96

Chapter Twelve
Into the Future 110

Timeline 120

Glossary 122

Bibliography 124

Index 126

Bill Gates (*AP/Wide World Photos*)

Chapter One

Trey

William Henry Gates III was born in Seattle, Washington on October 28, 1955. His grandmother Adelle, a fervent bridge player, thought that was too much name for a little boy. She dubbed him Trey, slang for a three card.

It is prophetic that Bill's nickname came from bridge, a game of chance. As an adult he would prove to be one of the biggest gamblers in American business. Winning most of his bets has made him the wealthiest individual in America.

The other ingredients of his success, in addition to luck, have been hard work, persistence, and an intense competitiveness. Gates is determined to win with every new venture he attempts. As he has grown older, it has also become apparent that he is driven by a sense of his place in history. He began his company in 1975, almost a century after John D. Rockefeller, probably the most famous and hated businessman in American history, started his oil company. Rockefeller's reign as the world's wealthiest, and most feared, tycoon stretched well into the twentieth century. At this early stage in the twenty-first century, Bill Gates is world famous. Another similarity between the two is that, as in the case of Rockefeller, the U.S. government has charged Gates with attempting to control an entire industry by building a monopoly and has taken him to court in an attempt to break up his empire. Gates is an important and controversial tycoon, and one of the most fascinating characters in the world of business today.

Bill's maternal great-grandfather, James Willard Maxwell, moved to the state of Washington in the late nineteenth century. Shortly after his arrival, Maxwell became the president and chief stockholder of a bank, served two terms as mayor of his hometown, and was elected to the state legislature. When Maxwell moved to Seattle shortly before World War I, he became one of the most prominent bankers in the growing metropolis.

Bill's great-grandfather exhibited the personality traits that continue to characterize the Maxwell family, including Bill's mother. Bill's father, Bill Gates Jr., was also from an ambitious family. Although the Gates family had not amassed as much wealth as the Maxwell family, they had lived in the Seattle area an even longer period of time, and had invested in a variety of successful businesses.

Bill Gates Jr. served as a second lieutenant during World War II. After the war he completed his undergraduate degree at the University of Washington and

The career of Bill Gates has often been compared to that of John D. Rockefeller, the nineteenth-century oil baron. *(Courtesy of the Rockefeller Archive Center.)*

began law school. Mary Maxwell, nicknamed "Giggles" by her sorority sisters, was a lively and active coed. While earning excellent grades, she participated in intramural sports and other extracurricular activities.

Bill Gates Jr. and Mary Maxwell were married in 1951. Bill joined a prominent Seattle law firm, while Mary taught school for a few years until they began their family. A daughter, Kristanne, was born in 1953, and two years later Trey was born. It would be nine years before the third and last Gates child, Libby, was born.

From the beginning, little Trey was a high-energy child. As a baby he grew impatient waiting for an adult to rock his cradle, so he learned how to rotate his body and make the cradle swing. Later, Mary discovered that sitting Trey on a rocking horse was the best way to entertain him. He would rock for hours. Incessant motion is still one of Bill's most noticeable characteristics.

From a very early age, Trey showed an independence of mind that his parents found challenging. When they finally decided to stop trying to control his behavior there was more peace in the family. For example, after years of struggling with him to pick up his clothes and clean his room, his mother made him an offer. She would stop complaining about his room if he promised to keep the door closed at all times.

One of the biggest events of Trey's childhood was the 1962 Seattle World's Fair. The Gates family visited every exhibit. The symbol of the fair, the Space Needle, is still one of Seattle's most prominent landmarks, complete with its revolving restaurant. Most of the exhibits were futuristic visions of how technology would change the world in the years to come. The space exhibit was sponsored by NASA and featured astronaut Alan Shepard, who had recently become the first American in space.

Also exhibiting at the fair was computer giant IBM (*I*nternational *B*usiness *M*achines). Big Blue, as IBM was called, set up a bank of giant computers programmed to translate languages. General Electric (G.E.) made the outrageous claim that in the future individuals would be able to make their own movies and watch them on giant, wall-sized color televisions, and that small computers for the home would take care of many chores. The fax machine, electronic mail, and computers capable of communicating without human intervention were all predicted at the 1962 World's Fair.

The early sixties was a period of optimism about science and technology. Motivated primarily by fear of the Soviet Union, American schools were encouraged to focus more attention on science and math to help the nation maintain its technological edge. This emphasis played to Bill's strongest talents.

"[Bill] was a nerd before the term was invented," is how one of his former teachers remembers him. His earliest love was math. When it came time for math drills he was always ahead of his classmates. This sometimes led to trouble. A bored Bill was prone to disrupt others. Bill was small for his age, hopelessly clumsy, with big feet and ears, and his parents even considered holding him back for a year. They hoped the extra time would allow him to mature, and help his grades in such things as conduct and penmanship. But they soon realized Trey's problem was not immaturity—it was boredom.

To combat the boredom, his parents encouraged Trey to learn outside of the classroom. They bought a new edition of the *World Book Encyclopedia,* but he quickly read through the entire set.

Another favorite activity was reading science fiction. Bill has spoken often of how exciting it was as a boy to read about the future as imagined by Isaac Asimov, Robert Heinlein, Arthur C. Clarke, and other favorite writers. At this stage in his life Bill planned to be a scientist, and the stories of faster-than-light travel and alien contact were tailor-made to excite a boy like Trey.

Like many in his family, Bill is intensely competitive. Card games, board games, even jigsaw puzzles, often turned into fierce battles. Bill did not like to lose, and would occasionally create friction by not losing gracefully. To this day, Bill Gates is not a good loser.

The Gates family attended University Congregational Church. Although Trey was more interested in science than religion, he found a way to show off his intelligence in Sunday school. Every year Reverend Dale Turner offered a free dinner at the restaurant sitting atop the Space Needle to any boy or girl who could memorize the entire Sermon on the Mount. The recitation took twenty-five minutes, and few of Turner's charges made the effort—although dinner at the Space Needle was an enticing prize. Not only did Bill attempt the memorization feat, he succeeded so well that Reverend Turner still remembers the day he sat in the Gates' family living room and listened to eleven-year-old Bill: "I needed only to go to his home that day to know that he was something special. I couldn't imagine how an eleven-year-old boy could have a mind like that. And my subsequent questioning of him revealed a deep understanding of the passage."

Early in life Bill showed an aptitude for business. One example of his emerging business savvy was a contract he designed, at age eleven, to give him access to his sister's baseball glove. The contract read: "When Trey wants the mitt, he gets it." He also included lines at the bottom for signatures. Although his father was a highly skilled attorney, and Trey no doubt learned most of his legalese from his dad, the fact that he wrote the contract, and the one-sided terms of the arrangement, are good indicators of the type of businessman Trey would become.

Examples of Bill's precociousness as a young boy have now become legend. While still in grade school, he wrote a fourteen-page report on the human body in less than an hour. When the teachers suggested he work with the librarian to help locate lost books, Bill became so involved in the project he had to be forced to go outside for recess.

Despite Trey's obvious intelligence, his parents were concerned. By the time he was in sixth grade, they were making frequent trips to the Laurelhurst Elementary School for parent-teacher-principal conferences, usually related to some prank Bill had pulled.

Bill's parents encouraged him to join the Boy Scouts. Despite his small size, Bill made an excellent scout, eventually earning Eagle Scout status. But scouting was not enough. Bill and Mary Gates realized Trey needed constant challenges. Already bored with the pace of regular schools, they feared continual boredom might make him lose interest in education altogether. They decided to send him to a private school.

Although his parents were thinking of Bill's future when they decided to send him to the exclusive Lakeside Preparatory School, it is doubtful they knew how fateful their decision was. Shortly after Bill's arrival on campus, the school leaders made an investment that did more than any other single event to determine the direction of Bill Gates's future. They leased a computer.

Chapter Two

Lakeside

At first, Bill resisted going to Lakeside. He even threatened to fail the entrance examination on purpose. But his parents knew that was an idle threat—he was not the type of boy to fail a test.

Bill was small for his age in the autumn of 1967, when he began the new school. He usually wore his shirt buttoned to his neck, and his extra long feet hung comically from his skinny legs. Despite his parent's efforts to get him interested in team sports, Bill spent most of his time in solitary pursuits, such as reading or just sitting around thinking.

At Lakeside, Bill became a member of the math and science group. His grades were only average, or slightly above, in most subjects. But in math he soon earned a reputation as the smartest boy in his class.

Although Bill did not seem to fit into the culture of the late 1960s, with its emphasis on being cool and hip, it would be a mistake to think that the turbulent era failed to influence his life. The youth culture of those years advocated a high level of personal freedom. Bill fully adopted the idea that the individual should be free to pursue his or her own destiny. This emphasis on personal freedom was important to many of the people who participated in the development of the microcomputer. What could be more personally liberating than millions of people having access to information that once had been reserved for a select few?

Bill was not the only boy at Lakeside interested in math and science. There, he made friends with Kent Evans, the son of a Unitarian minister. In addition to his enthusiasm for the same subjects as Bill, Kent brought something else to the friendship. Kent wanted to make money—lots of money. One of the teachers at the school said Kent "acted like a forty-year-old businessman." Years later, Bill's father remarked that a great deal of his son's instinct for business came from Kent Evans.

During the summer vacation of 1968, Lakeside's administrators decided to find a way for the students to have access to a computer. They were attempting to keep the boys on the cutting edge of a rapidly changing technology.

The computer revolution that has done so much to alter the way we work and play began to gain steam during the 1960s. At the beginning of that turbulent decade, computers were huge, complicated machines few people could understand or operate. The dominant power in the industry was IBM. IBM had grown into one of the world's largest corporations by selling giant main-

Paul Allen (seated) and Bill Gates in the Lakeside computer room. *(Lakeside School)*

frame computers. The machines sold for millions of dollars, demanded constant maintenance, and had only a fraction of the power of a present-day laptop.

During the 1960s, motivated by the Cold War and the race to put a United States astronaut on the moon by the end of the decade, giant advances were made in computer technology. While IBM was wedded to expensive mainframes, which generated big profits, other companies worked to make computing more affordable. The first company that focused on making smaller, less expensive computers was Digital Equipment Corporation. Digital's entry into this new world of minicomputers, which were approximately the size of the average refrigerator, was the PDP (*P*rogram *D*ata *P*rocessor) series.

Another advancement in the 1960s was more a business arrangement than a technological breakthrough. Because of the expense of computers, entrepreneurs hit upon the idea of leasing computer time. This new arrangement greatly increased the number of people who could access and utilize this new technology.

Lakeside leased computer time from a number of companies in Seattle. To communicate with the rented computer, Lakeside invested in an ASR-33 Teletype. At the time teletypes were used mostly in newsrooms. Noisy, with clacking keys, the teletype combined a keyboard, printer, paper tape puncher (paper tapes stored data before the introduction of floppy disks), and a modem that clapped around both ends of a telephone receiver to send information over phone lines to the leased computer.

Bill was one of the students most enthusiastic about

accessing the computer. Lakeside did not offer computing courses because none of the faculty had enough computer experience to do so. But a few teachers knew enough to introduce the interested boys to the mysterious machines. One of them remembers Bill. "It took him a week to pass me [in computer knowledge]," the teacher said.

Although the boys hanging around Lakeside's computer room were enthusiastic about all aspects of computing, they divided into two groups—those who were more interested in the hardware, the actual machine, and those more interested in the software, or programming. Bill and Kent Evans were drawn toward software and programming. Paul Allen, two years older than Bill and Kent, was attracted to the hardware.

Computing was much more difficult in the late 1960s than it is today. To use a computer successfully it was necessary to know a programming language. The most accessible language was BASIC (*B*eginner's *A*ll-purpose *S*ymbolic *I*nstruction *C*ode). The commands in BASIC have commonsense names like RUN, LIST, GoTo, etc. Bill set out to master BASIC, and was soon writing programs that could solve math problems or play Tic-Tac-Toe.

Renting computer time was expensive and quickly depleted the school's computing budget. Then a wonderful thing happened. A new company called the Computer Center Corporation (quickly dubbed C-Cubed by the math crowd) opened. This was the first company in Seattle attempting to make a profit by renting computer time. More importantly, it installed the new state-of-the-art PDP-10, manufactured by Digital Equipment.

One of the owners of C-Cubed had a son at Lakeside, and she knew about the eager computer whizzes there. C-Cubed needed their help. At that time, computers were sold with an extended up-front period that allowed the customer to test the machine and make sure it operated as advertised. The management of C-Cubed wanted to run their new PDP-10 through a strenuous shakedown. Who better to put the computer through its paces than the energetic group of hackers at Lakeside? The company offered Bill and his friends free computer time every weekend. In return the boys had to promise to try to make the machine crash—to find out which combinations of commands caused the computer to stop working—and to record all crashes. Most crashes were caused by hardware or software glitches that have been called "bugs" since 1945, when a moth created a malfunction in a highly expensive, experimental mainframe computer at Harvard University. The company wanted the bugs located so they could be fixed before it was time to begin making payments.

The boys were enthusiastic about free computer time. And their job was to make the system crash. It was like a computer demolition derby. Bill quickly emerged as the best crasher in the group, not that crashing a PDP-10 was particularly difficult. Most of the mistakes made on today's computers result in error messages. But on the PDP-10 almost every error, such as entering too long a string of characters at a prompt, resulted in a crash. In

Bill spent many long hours in the Lakeside computer room. *(Lakeside School)*

other words, a crash was the PDP-10's version of an error message. Of course, the problem with this system was that more than one person could be using the computer at the same time. C-Cubed had eight teletypes hardwired to the unit, and other customers communicated via modem. When a crash occurred it knocked everyone off the system, and all work in progress was lost.

Bill, however, soon grew tired of crashing the machine. He focused on programming and learning more about computer langues. Using BASIC, he wrote an elaborate war game. Paul Allen remembers the game as taking up "fifty feet of Teletype paper." Bill never finished the program. He kept adding new features, clearly more interested in designing the game and writing the code than he was in the finished product. This willingness to experiment to make his program more complex would serve him well later.

Bill's obsession with the computer grew. Soon he was sneaking out of his house at night and riding the bus back to C-Cubed. Interestingly, Bill's grades improved as his interest in computers increased. Concentrating harder on one part of his life seemed to help the other. His parents, it seemed, had been right. Their son's worst enemy was boredom.

Bill was never merely a hacker, though. His friendship with Kent Evans, and later with Paul Allen, had another common element besides their shared interest in computers. All three boys were also interested in making money.

By Bill's junior year at Lakeside, C-Cubed was out of business. The company's plans to make a fortune by renting computer time had never materialized. Making a profit out of the new technology was not as easy as they had hoped. But Bill was undeterred. He told anyone who would listen that he was going to make a million dollars by age thirty. It was one of the few times on record that Bill Gates underestimated himself.

Chapter Three

Teenage Programmer

After C-Cubed closed, Bill and his friends formed the Lakeside Programmers Group. The organization was dedicated to finding computer time and discovering a way for the teenagers to make some money. Paul Allen, who was by now in his freshman year at Washington State University, located a PDP-10 on campus. That was all it took to convince the boys to move their operations there. Although Paul was the only university student in the group, and Bill looked several years younger than his actual age, the professors responsible for the computers quickly learned that the boys were a valuable asset to have around.

Not long after the group was formed, another computer timesharing company, located in Portland, Oregon, asked Paul Allen to write a payroll program. Initially, Paul tried to write the program without the help of Bill and Kent Evans, but he was in over his head. A payroll program had many different modules, and demanded

knowledge of taxes, deductions, and other business tech-
nicalities. To further complicate matters, the company
insisted the program be written in COBOL (*CO*mmon
*B*usiness-*O*riented *L*anguage), a language Paul did not
know.

No one was quicker to learn new computer languages
than Bill. Soon Bill and Kent were doing most of the
work on the payroll project.

Although the two boys agreed to work with Paul, they
were angry that he had initially tried to leave them out of
the project. Before beginning work, Bill and Kent insisted the group formalize their relationship. Bill's father
drew up a formal partnership that protected each boy's
interests. Bill had learned from Paul's attempt to exclude
him that he had to protect his own interests in business. It
was not a lesson he needed to learn twice.

After Bill and Kent started work, Paul backed out. He
could not go to college and work on the software at the
same time. In the years to come both Paul and Bill would
have to face the same decision: Pursue their dream of
owning a software company or continue their education?
This time Paul decided to focus on college.

Bill and Kent plowed on with the work. As Paul
remembered years later, "They [Bill and Kent] worked
really hard on that thing." In the middle of the work the
timesharing company threatened to break the contract.
Apparently, Bill and Kent had over-promised on delivery
time, and the company complained that the software had
too many bugs. Bill and Kent took a train to Portland to
patch over the problems—then doubled their efforts to

hurry the writing of code and still make it as error-free as possible. This is another early example of Bill Gates' working style: over-promise to get the bid, and let the customers find the bugs for themselves.

In the end, Bill and Kent finished the project and were paid with $10,000 worth of computer time. There was a catch, though: the time had to be spent in less than a year.

Bill and Kent soon put their opportunity to work. Lakeside had recently merged with an all-girls' school. The influx of new students created a scheduling nightmare. Why not take advantage of the chaos and put the scheduling on computer? The school put a math teacher in charge, and Bill and Kent began work.

Tragedy soon struck when the math teacher was killed in a plane crash. The accident left no one except Bill and Kent to finish the job. The school offered to pay them, so, just as they had on the payroll contract, the boys worked day and night writing code. The free computer time they had earned meant they could pocket all the money they would make from Lakeside.

The boys worked so many hours they began sleeping in the teachers' lounge. Bill was already famous for his disregard of such time-wasters as taking baths and combing his hair. His physical appearance deteriorated even further.

Then, tragedy struck again. Kent left the project for a few days to take a beginner's mountain-climbing class. While crossing a snow field, the exhausted Kent Evans fell over 600 feet to his death.

Bill was shattered. One of Lakeside's teachers at the

time was Robert Fulghum, who would later become a best-selling author of self-help books. Fulghum was also a minister, and he presided over Kent's funeral service. After the service, Bill broke into tears.

But the project had to go on. Bill recruited Paul Allen to take Kent's place. While working on the project, Bill and Paul became closer than ever. The age difference had seemed greater when Bill was a scrawny seventh grader and Paul was a tall, mature-beyond-his-years upperclassman. Now the gap seemed insignificant. Bill likely needed a new close friend after Kent's sudden death. He and Paul, while racing against the clock to finish the program for Lakeside, also forged a working relationship that would eventually turn both into billionaires.

The class schedule was completed on time, and sixteen-year-old Bill earned $4,200. The scheduling program secured Bill's reputation as the smartest boy on campus. Over the years, as his fame has grown internationally, Bill has used the story in interviews. He laughs and says that because he maintained the program for the rest of his time at Lakeside, he always got every class he wanted. He even claims to have used the software to arrange a history class made up entirely of girls—except for one skinny boy named Bill Gates.

Bill spent part of the summer between his junior and senior years working as a congressional page in the U. S. House of Representatives. Here, another Bill Gates legend was born. The year was 1972, and there was a presidential campaign between then president Richard Nixon, who was running for reelection, and Democratic

Senator George McGovern. McGovern initially selected Missouri Senator Thomas Eagleton as his running mate. Scandal erupted when the media discovered that Eagleton had been under the care of a psychiatrist for years, and had undergone electroshock therapy for depression. McGovern dropped Eagleton from the ticket.

This change made the campaign buttons that read McGovern/Eagleton obsolete. Bill thought these seemingly useless items would become very valuable to collectors, and would soon be worth much more than their current price. He supposedly bought as many of the campaign buttons as possible, and later sold them at a profit. The story has been disputed, but there is no way to know for certain whether or not it really happened. It is worth noting, though, that Bill's legend always seems to swirl around making money—not solving some intricate software problem. Although he was a talented, maybe even gifted programmer, it is in business that Bill Gates uses his full potential.

Shortly after Bill returned home to Seattle from his summer in Washington, D.C., he and Paul formed a new company. They named their new enterprise Traf-O-Data.

Paul was beginning his second year at Washington State University, where he was majoring in Computer Science. He was tiring of school and wanted to start a business. An avid reader of electronics magazines, Paul was excited to learn that Intel, a California company specializing in the design and production of computer microprocessors, had released its most powerful chip yet—the 8008.

The processor is the brain of any computer. Intel, and

other companies, had been working toward making the processor smaller and less expensive. These new processors, which integrated millions of circuits into a tiny silicon chip, were dubbed microprocessors. Intel's first microprocessor, the 4004, was a disappointment to computer enthusiasts because of its tiny capacity. The 4004 could not sustain even the smallest program, and was eventually used in the home appliance market. But the new 8008 chip was more promising. Paul and Bill thought they could build a new company around the 8008.

Bill already had a full schedule, which should have left him little time to start a business. He was a senior at Lakeside, and was busy applying to the nation's best colleges. But he decided to form a partnership with Paul, and to try to make a success of their new company.

Traf-O-Data was based on a novel idea. At that time, most cities maintained records of traffic flow by stretching a rubber hose across the designated streets. When a car passed over the hose, a binary message was sent to a metal box that punched either a zero or a one, to correlate time and volume, onto a paper tape. At the end of the day, the data had to be translated into information the city or county could use when making decisions about such things as traffic light synchronization and new road construction.

Paul and Bill's idea was to use the new 8008 chip to create a machine that could "read" the paper tapes much more quickly than was presently possible. The original idea was to write a program using BASIC. The program would read the tape. However, even the new 8008 microprocessor was not powerful enough to support a program written in BASIC. This would not be the last time Bill's software ideas would outstrip existing hardware capabilities.

This early business venture is interesting particularly for one point. Although Bill and Paul would go on to make their fortune in software, the most successful part of the Traf-O-Data scheme was the small computer they had built to process the tapes.

The two friends, after forming the company, purchased one of the 8008 microprocessors for $360. While Paul and Bill used the PDP-10 at Lakeside to write the code necessary to make the machine work, they hired an electrical engineer to build the machine. Eventually, they created the Traf-O-Data box, a primitive microcomputer that could be connected to a tape reader to collect the information. While the processor was not powerful enough to run software, it could support the one function it was designed to perform—reading the tapes supplied by traffic departments.

The next task for the young entrepreneurs was to find customers. They wrote to traffic departments all over the United States and Canada to solicit business. Eventually, they contracted with a few municipalities in the Northwestern U.S., Canada, and as far away as Maryland, to read their traffic tapes and send back the information.

Traf-O-Data was not a big success, however. Bill was preparing for college and did not have time to run a company and Paul was already busy with his university workload. But the Traf-O-Data experience provided both

Bill and Paul their first opportunity to start a business from the ground up, and to invest some of their money. It was a key initial step into the world of entrepreneurship. Perhaps most importantly, their experience with the 8008 microprocessor would turn out to be extremely valuable three years later when the long-awaited microcomputer revolution finally got off the ground.

Chapter Four

Harvard

Despite all the time he was spending with his first love, computers, Bill's grades improved every year he was at Lakeside. It was as though having a new focus outside the classroom motivated him to do better work in the classroom. He even won a National Merit Scholarship his senior year. He was also popular with his teachers, and envied by most of the other students. Bill was considered by most to be the smartest and most motivated young man on campus. It was an honor Bill worked hard to attain, and he was not shy about letting people know it. Though he was always eager to win the approval of others, he managed to anger some students. More than one boy challenged the skinny guy with glasses and a long nose to a fight. They were usually angry about something he had said; or maybe he had laughed at someone for not answering a question in class as quickly as Bill thought he should. It was this intellectual arrogance that some of Bill's fellow students disliked about him.

In the last trimester of Bill's senior year of high school, he and Paul left Seattle for Vancouver, in the Canadian province of British Columbia. TRW, the giant defense contractor, had hired them to write software for a project desperately behind schedule. Paul dropped out of college, and Bill received permission to miss the remainder of the school year. While at TRW, Bill became an even better programmer, working under the guidance of managers who had been in the business for years.

Bill returned to Lakeside in time to take his final exams. He aced most of his classes, and graduated from Lakeside with honors.

After graduation, Bill returned to Vancouver to finish the project for TRW. He and Paul shared an apartment, and spent the hours not devoted to writing software exploring the city or talking over their dream of one day owning their own software company. But Bill told Paul those plans would have to wait. He was going to Harvard in the fall, and his parents would never allow him to pass up a chance to attend one of the country's most prestigious universities to start a business in the risky computer software industry.

Bill arrived at Harvard, located in Cambridge, Massachusetts, in the fall of 1973. He was not yet eighteen. Although he had been accepted at several engineering schools, he had decided to study math. To the competitive Bill, anyone could be an engineer. He considered math the subject for the smartest people.

But, as Bill himself admitted later, he soon discovered there were students at Harvard who were better mathematicians than he was. Although he was very good, he was not the best. This revelation bruised his ego, and helped persuade him that fame—and fortune—lay outside of academia.

Initially, Bill dove into the undergraduate experience with the same energy he used in his other pursuits. He signed up for Math 55, which only accepted the brightest first-year students. He also took the typical mixture of introductory courses in English, history, chemistry, and physics.

Bill had an active life outside the classroom. He became a regular in the all-night poker games in his dormitory. Surprisingly, considering the bluffing skills he later developed in the business world, Bill was only an average poker player, as likely to lose as he was to win.

Soon after settling down on campus, Bill began visiting Aiken Hall, the campus computer center. Although he had not yet taken the university-required computer courses, he pushed himself to the forefront of the university hackers. Before long he was using the more powerful machines reserved for graduate students. The director of the computer center remembered Gates well: "He was a helluva good programmer." "But," the professor continued, "he's an obnoxious human being." As had been the case at Lakeside, several people were offended by Bill's impatience and his tendency to put others down unnecessarily.

A friend of Bill's back in Seattle had recently designed *Spacewar,* one of the first computer games. One of Bill's computer projects at Harvard was the development of a video baseball game. He never completed the baseball game, though, primarily because he kept adding features.

Bill gained notoriety at Harvard for other characteristics besides his intelligence and impatience, especially his lack of interest in creature comforts and clothes. His entire life was computers, poker, and school. Once, while he was working day and night on a program, his roommate discovered Bill asleep, fully dressed, mumbling "One, comma, one, comma, one." Bill was writing computer code in his dreams.

Such an intense lifestyle had a price. After his first year, Bill became ill with an intestinal problem, and spent most of the summer of 1974 sick in Seattle.

When Bill returned to Harvard in the fall, much of the steam went out of his drive for a degree. There was no denying any longer that his focus was on business, not academia. He attended college for two more years, but there is little evidence that he pursued life in Cambridge as intensely as he had during his first year. This was partly due to his growing doubts that formal education was what he wanted—or needed—in order to have the type of life he desired.

Bill's time at Harvard was spent trapped between two pressures. He was a student at one of America's best universities, which was something that gave him a sense of accomplishment. His parents were proud of him. He understood the advantages a Harvard degree could provide him later in life. On the other hand, he loved working with software. His experiences at TRW and Lakeside, and even the less successful venture with Traf-O-Data, had convinced him and Paul Allen that there was plenty of money to be made in the computer industry.

At that time, an exciting new development was coming out of Albuquerque, New Mexico—a development that would forever alter the future of the computer.

Chapter Five

BASIC Beginnings

The January 1975 issue of *Popular Electronics* magazine had a startling cover story:

PROJECT BREAKTHROUGH
WORLD'S FIRST MINICOMPUTER KIT
TO RIVAL COMMERCIAL MODELS. . .
"ALTAIR 8800"

The cover photograph was of a metal box with a front panel of lights and a row of toggle switches. The Altair 8800 did not have a keyboard or a monitor.

The tiny computer was manufactured by a small company called Micro Instrumentation and Telemetry Systems, or MITS. MITS had originally built electronic calculators, a highly profitable business in the early 1970s. But by the middle of the decade, the bottom had dropped out of the calculator market and Ed Roberts, the owner of MITS, decided to try something new. Roberts was convinced the new 8080 microprocessor from Intel, which was a great improvement over the 8008 chip Bill and Paul had used in the Traf-O-Data machine, was powerful enough to run a small computer.

The cover story in *Popular Electronics* was somewhat misleading. The Altair 8800 did not actually yet exist. For $397, the customer received a box of loose parts. It took several hours with a soldering gun, and some fairly advanced knowledge of electronics, to turn the box of parts into a computer.

Then there was the problem of what to do with the Altair 8800 after it was built. There was no software, there were no games, there was not even a language that programmers could use to write software. Essentially, it was an expensive box that blinked red lights.

Bill and Paul saw an opportunity. They knew that for the Altair to sell, languages had to be developed that would run on the tiny box. They read all about the 8080. It was more powerful that the 8008, but it was still a long way from the processor used in the PDP-10. This meant that only a small, modified version of a simple language, like BASIC, would have a chance of working on the Altair 8800.

There was another reason Bill wanted to make BASIC the first language for the Altair. BASIC was an easy language to learn and best suited to the talents of the young people excited about microcomputers.

During the years when great attention was paid to the more public advocates of social change, it was perhaps the technological advances of the time, such as small

Ed Roberts designed the Altair 8800, the first microcomputer to be sold at an inexpensive price. *(Seattle Post-Intelligencer)*

computers, inexpensive photocopiers, and other communication equipment, that did the most to empower individuals.

The new computers also provided opportunities to make money. Although they had not written the first line of code, Bill and Paul called Ed Roberts at MITS and told him they had a version of BASIC that would run on the Altair 8800. Roberts was more than a little skeptical—but he had a secret of his own. The Altair 8800 was still only a shell. It was not operable. Several hardware bugs needed to be worked out. He asked Bill and Paul to wait a month before visiting MITS headquarters. Hopefully, Roberts would have a working machine by then.

Bill and Paul faked disappointment and agreed to the delay. Then they hung up the phone and started a marathon programming session.

The 8080 chip had so little memory Bill had to write the code (the actual lines of instructions that make a program run) extremely tightly. To use the expression of the day, he had to "burn" the code, in other words, find a way for one line of instructions to perform as many functions as possible. There was no room in the limited memory for unnecessary commands. It was difficult work, but the two young men were excited.

They did most of the work at the Aiken Computer Lab. Because an Altair 8800 was not available, they made a PDP-10 mimic an Altair 8800. While Paul concentrated on tricking the PDP-10 into performing like a tiny computer, Bill concentrated on BASIC.

The two young men worked day and night. Desperate to finish, they recruited another student to help. The hours were grueling. They ate once a day, usually midnight pizza. Sleep came in short snatches stretched out on a table in the computer lab.

Finally, it was time to take the software to Albuquerque, New Mexico, where MITS was located. Paul made the trip because he was older and looked more mature. Bill still did not look old enough to drive, although he was nineteen.

Paul fretted during the entire plane ride. One bug could keep the entire program from working. He would be standing in front of Ed Roberts with a useless program. It was a long, nerve-wracking flight.

Paul's nervousness was considerably relieved when he arrived in New Mexico and saw the headquarters of MITS. The Altair 8800 was produced in a dilapidated one-story building. Both MITS and the computer whizzes from Harvard had exaggerated their own importance.

If Paul was disappointed by the MITS headquarters, he forgot it when he ran the paper tape containing the BASIC code through the Altair 8800, then entered instructions into the machine by carefully sequencing the toggle switches. Finally, the machine printed the prompt: "Memory size?" After Allen entered the correct answer, he asked the machine to add 2 + 2. When the Altair 8800 printed 4, Paul knew the code worked.

Ed Roberts and the other MITS executives were ecstatic. Suddenly, their little computer could do more than blink lights. There was actually a language that worked within the limited memory. This should have been what it took to make MITS a giant success. The fact that it did not had more to do with bad business management than with the quality of the product.

For the moment everyone was happy. MITS wanted to license Bill's adapted BASIC, and they offered Paul a job as vice-president in charge of software development. When Paul left Albuquerque a few days later, he took a functioning Altair 8800 home with him.

In April of 1975, MITS announced they were releasing BASIC for the Altair 8800. But even at this early stage of the relationship, problems developed. The biggest was that none of the computer kits MITS sold had enough memory to run the new BASIC correctly. In order to have enough RAM (*R*andom *A*ccess *M*emory)—the amount of memory capacity a computer has when it is running—the customer would have to pay extra for new boards that supposedly contained four kilobytes of RAM. However, many customers complained the new boards did not work.

Another problem developed over OEMs (*O*riginal *E*quipment *M*anufacturers), which would eventually be responsible for much of Microsoft's success. OEMs were companies who built similar, if not identical, products, such as the popular IBM compatible computers in the 1980s. In the agreement, Ed Roberts promised to help market the new BASIC to other computer companies. According to the terms of the deal, MITS would receive a commission for every copy they sold to OEMs.

Roberts, however, soon realized it would be better for him if the Altair 8800 was the only machine that ran BASIC. That way he would have a larger share of the market. Consequently, he was not motivated to sell the software.

These conflicts would grow over time. But shortly after making the deal Bill had another problem on his hands. He and Paul Allen had used the computers at Harvard in their efforts to modify BASIC. When the administration of the school discovered what they considered an unauthorized use of the school's computers, they began an investigation. The officials were particularly concerned that Bill had allowed non-student Paul Allen to use the Harvard computers, and that the machines had been used for the young men's personal profit.

Gates was called before the administrators. To this day, no one has spoken publicly about what sort of punishment he received. It is clear, however, that free use of Harvard computers was a thing of the past. Bill and Paul used some of the money they had earned from the MITS deal to rent computer time from a downtown Boston firm.

The conflict with the Harvard administration would be one of the final straws for Bill. The importance of Harvard had already been receding in Bill's mind and, after closing the deal with MITS, he felt the urge to move on more strongly than ever. MITS was anxious for more languages to be adapted to the small computer, and Bill recruited friends to help. Bill was also thinking beyond MITS. He knew that the computer was entering the mainstream of American life. He envisioned a future in which nearly every home had a computer, just as they had televisions. Bill wanted those computers to be running his software.

But in order to make money from software you have to keep ownership of your work. This was not always an easy task. Many hackers sneered at the idea of an individual controlling what they felt should be common knowledge. They considered it undemocratic and a violation of the hacker ethic. Bill, however, saw things differently. When he heard that computer groups in Northern California were using pirated copies of his BASIC— which meant he did not receive his royalty as provided for in the contract with MITS—he dashed off an angry letter to the MITS newsletter. In the letter, Bill vented his anger at the "thieves" who used unauthorized copies of his work. He also made Ed Roberts write a letter threatening to prosecute anyone caught using illegal copies. But again Bill and Roberts's interests diverged. It was to MITS's advantage for users to have the program because they made more money selling the hardware than they did the software. Roberts would have given the software away if it would make more people buy his computer kits.

Bill made enemies by the vigorous way he protected his "intellectual property." But perhaps he merely saw the future more clearly than most. Before the advent of personal computers, software was not usually sold on the open market. All the focus, and interest, was on the computer. Clearly, to Bill's mind, this was going to change. From the beginning of the microcomputer era, Bill realized that the computer was only as good as the software it ran. Both his love and his talent were in creating software, and he wanted to be certain that he would receive a return on his work.

Despite his concerns, Bill began working on a new, improved version of BASIC for a more powerful Altair 8800. But he was beginning to feel the effects of attending Harvard and writing commercial software at the same time. He was exhausted. It was time to make a decision he had been putting off for a long time. At last, he decided to quit Harvard.

His mother was firmly opposed to the idea, and searched for some way to change his mind. When Bill visited Seattle to tell his family about his decision to leave school, she asked a family friend to take Bill to lunch and talk him out of leaving college.

Mary Gates should have picked a better person to change Bill's mind. The family friend was a self-made multimillionaire who had never finished college. During the lunch, when he was supposed to be convincing Bill to remain in school, he found himself growing more and more enthusiastic as Bill elaborated on his plans to move to Albuquerque, where he and Paul would formalize their working relationship into a software company. Bill explained why software was going to be the fastest growing industry in the second half of the twentieth century. Before the lunch was over, the family friend told Bill he thought he was doing the right thing. Mary Gates was not happy. Years later, the man joked that he should have given Bill a blank check, so he could have been in on one of the most successful business start-ups in history.

Chapter Six

Microsoft

Microsoft was originally spelled Micro-Soft when Bill and Paul formed the company in the summer of 1975. But the hyphenated name is known to have been used only once, in an advertisement in the MITS newsletter. Throughout the company's history it has been known as Microsoft—a combination of micro, indicating microcomputers, and soft, indicating software.

Originally Bill insisted that he own sixty percent of the business because he had done most of the work on the Altair BASIC. Later, Bill was able to increase his share of the company to sixty-four percent. Bill has always claimed that none of his family's money was ever invested in Microsoft. He was determined to be a success on his own.

Although his family did not give him money, they had already given him something more valuable. Working hard, even working excessively hard, was a Gates family trait that Bill applied to Microsoft. Later, Bill would have more than one girlfriend grow weary of his long hours. Another Gates family trait was frugality. Bill Gates reportedly still flies coach. To fly first class would be "decadent," a word Bill reserves for anything he finds distasteful.

Microsoft was originally formed in Albuquerque. Early on, both Bill and Paul saw their new company's future tied to the success of MITS. Later, extracting themselves from MITS' clutches would create the first of many legal challenges Microsoft would face.

After moving to New Mexico, Bill began developing a new version of BASIC that would run on the new, more powerful computer MITS was developing. He also worked on fixing bugs in the earlier version.

Bill and Paul needed some help. Where better to turn for help than to the other young hackers they had known at Lakeside and Harvard? Bill lured the boys—Microsoft was at first very much a young man's company—to Albuquerque, where they slept on the floor of the apartment Bill and Paul shared. Their days and nights consisted of cranking out code and testing it on the computer time they rented from the city's school system. One of the early Microsoft hackers remembers those days as "almost a missionary kind of work in the sense that we were delivering something to someone they never thought they could have. There was a kinship that you wouldn't normally see in a commercial enterprise."

After a summer of intense work, the new BASIC was up and running. But the new computer was behind schedule. Bill became convinced he had made a mistake by linking Microsoft so closely to MITS when he attended the First Annual World Altair Computer Convention in Albuquerque in March of 1976. The convention was filled with hackers, many of whom had ordered computers that had never arrived. Others were angry about the computer's faulty memory expansion boards. Mismanagement at MITS was frustrating its core of customer support, and the inevitable was happening. New companies were building better small computers. But Microsoft could only sell the BASIC designed to run on the 8080 microprocessor to MITS. In other words, unless MITS sold BASIC to these new OEMs, Microsoft was cut out of doing business in this new industry. And MITS did not see how helping out competing computer manufacturers could possibly be in its own best interest.

Bill decided to avoid this problem in the future. The new BASIC was designed to run on a more powerful processor, the 6800. This time, instead of selling the rights to MITS, Bill insisted on a non-exclusive licensing agreement. Microsoft would receive a fee when the program went out "bundled" with MITS hardware. But Microsoft remained free to license the program to any other computer manufacturer. These were the basic parameters of the deals Microsoft would make in the future.

This new strategy in hand, Bill began traveling the country selling Microsoft's new products. He wrote promotional letters, made calls to computer companies, and bought advertisements in computer newsletters. He also attended every conference possible. The name Microsoft quickly became well known in the industry.

Bill and the new employees began adapting other programming languages for small computers. In the company's first years, the vast majority of its income came from this type of product. It would not be until the early 1980s that Bill realized more and more computer users were not computer programmers. These general users needed software they could install in their machines and use—not languages to be used to write programs. Among the languages Microsoft attempted to modify for the smaller microprocessors were APL, COBOL, FORTRAN, and a little-used language first developed by Digital Equipment called FOCAL.

It was around 1976 that Bill first heard of a garage start-up computer company based in the San Francisco Bay Area of California. Apple Computer was the brainchild of Steve Jobs and Steve Wozniak, and it was using a new microprocessor called the 6502, manufactured by a small California company. Apple turned down the opportunity to buy BASIC with the comment they could write their own, better version. It would not be the last time Microsoft and Apple found themselves operating at cross-purposes.

Microsoft's first big break after MITS came from another former calculator maker, Commodore International. Commodore announced the upcoming release of the Personal Electronic Transactor (PET). The Commodore PET wanted the Microsoft BASIC to be installed on their ROM (Read Only Memory) chip. This meant that when the computer was turned on, a BASIC prompt would appear on the screen. If the user could master the

BASIC commands, the PET could be used to write letters or do calculations.

The PET, which came with 64K of memory, also had a keyboard and monitor attached. With the closing of the Commodore deal, Microsoft began signing contracts with most of the other new computer companies, as well as older companies such as General Electric. Microsoft was already a highly profitable enterprise.

Microsoft now had so much work they had to move to larger quarters in downtown Albuquerque. It was during this period that Bill started reciting the slogan that later became famous within the company: *A computer in every home, and Microsoft software on every computer.*

Things were certainly looking up. Then trouble struck. Pertac Computer Corporation bought MITS for $6 million. Pertac was even more determined than MITS not to uphold the agreement to find customers willing to license the BASIC written for the Altair 8800. Furthermore, it insisted Microsoft did not have the right to license the software to any other company. Pertac claimed all rights to the BASIC that Bill and Paul had originally written for the 8080 microprocessor, which was still Microsoft's most valuable product.

In April of 1977, Microsoft sent Pertac a letter listing itscomplaints. It accused the company of failing to live up to its side of the agreement. Pertac, which had revenues of $100 million, decided to put the young upstarts in their place. They filed suit to stop Microsoft from sharing the BASIC 8080 source code with any other company. If Pertac's legal action succeeded, it could be

Apple Computer co-founder Steve Jobs designed the Macintosh to be the first user friendly personal computer. *(AP/Wide World Photos)*

devastating for Microsoft because the other companies who had ordered the source code refused to pay until they saw how the litigation was resolved.

Some at Microsoft wanted to cave in to Pertac's demands. They saw nothing but disaster resulting from the fight. But Bill refused to give up.

Finally, just as the company was dangerously strapped for cash, the court decided that MITS and Pertac had not lived up to their part of the agreement. Microsoft was free to sell the 8080 source code to anyone willing to pay the price. The ties to MITS were broken.

Customers rolled in. Radio Shack joined Commodore in adding BASIC to its ROM chip, and several overseas companies, especially from Japan, placed orders.

Bill and Paul decided it was time to move. They were only in New Mexico because that was where MITS had been located. They both missed the northwest; Bill especially missed his family. After considering joining the dozens of other companies that were locating in Silicon Valley, outside of San Francisco, Bill and Paul decided to return to Seattle. They wanted their own identity, and thought it would be easier to establish and maintain it if they were not so close to others in the industry.

In January 1978, Microsoft opened its new, rented headquarters in an office building in Bellevue, Washington, a suburb of Seattle. By the mid-1980s, Microsoft would outgrow the Bellevue location, and move to a huge, multi-building campus in Redmond, another Seattle suburb. By that time Microsoft would be the fastest-growing corporation in America.

Chapter Seven

DOS

From the first day employees went to work at Microsoft they learned two things. The atmosphere was informal—no one wore a tie, for example—and Bill Gates was the most demanding boss they would ever have. "Bill was always pushing," is how one programmer remembers the early days. "We would do something I thought was very clever, and he would say 'Why don't you do this, or why didn't you do that two days ago?' That would get frustrating sometimes." It was not uncommon to hear Bill yell, "That's the stupidest thing I've ever heard." Working for Bill Gates was not always pleasant. He wasted little time worrying about the feelings of those who worked for him, and he drove them incessantly.

He drove himself even harder. He even joked about what he called his seven-hour turnaround: Leave the office late at night, go home, eat, sleep, and be back in the office only seven hours later. Bill was proud of his seven-hour turn around, and expected his employees to show the same dedication. Some could stand the pressure, and even thrived on it. Others could not.

In the early years of Microsoft, most of the workers stayed for one reason. Beginning with the Altair 8800, the microcomputer was coming into its own. In a few years, *Time* magazine would not select a man or woman as its Person of the Year. Instead, the prominent news magazine selected the personal computer as the Machine of the Year. The long-awaited computer revolution had begun, and like most revolutions, the young were leading it.

Digital Equipment had begun the move toward more affordable computers with its PDP series, and the copier company Xerox had become legendary for all the technological advances it was making at its Palo Alto Research Center (PARC) facility. But the rapid development of the microcomputer—small enough to sit on a desk and inexpensive enough for small businesses and even individuals to own—was fast creating an entirely new industry. Because Bill Gates and Paul Allen had been so quick to respond with software for the new machines, Microsoft had a strategic head start over the thousands of other programmers eager to cash in on this new market.

From the beginning, Microsoft was the dominant force in programming languages. In the first years, Bill forged a simple strategy. They concentrated on rewriting languages originally created for the mainframe market, such as COBOL, for the microcomputer market. It was this rapid movement into the language business that laid the foundation for the company's success.

Computer languages are used by programmers to write programs. In the late 1970s and early 1980s there was little retail off-the-shelf software available. This meant that unless the person buying the computer could get software made custom for his or her machine, it was practically useless. Most of the programs were written for specific, narrow tasks. For example, if a small distributing company wanted to computerize its inventory, it could hire someone to write a program to handle that specific need. Initially, Bill and most of the others in the business thought this was the way the microcomputer would be used. He saw little market for off-the-shelf software. Besides, who wanted to deal with people who did not know the difference between RAM and ROM? Bill, who prided himself on his intelligence, and who had a company made up of smart, computer-savvy people, did not want to be in the business of educating the computer-illiterate public. Focusing on languages meant that Microsoft did not have to spend time supporting its products.

Things were changing, however, whether Bill liked it or not. Bright programmers realized that a program that could be used to handle ordinary tasks, such as word processing, would sell thousands, maybe even millions of copies. Software would become a commodity, like automobiles or cereal.

On July 21, 1980, Bill Gates received a phone call that would drastically change Microsoft's future—moving him and his company into the highest echelons of American business.

IBM, the largest computer maker in the world, had decided to enter the microcomputer market. It was not an easy decision for the company to make. Highly expensive mainframes had turned the company into a multibillion dollar enterprise. Whether or not the king of giant computers should enter the low-end, relatively low-profit area of microcomputers was an argument that embroiled the directors for several years. Finally, the advocates of an IBM microcomputer won the battle.

Because of the amount of time it took to make a decision, the managers of the IBM personal computer project had to play catch-up. Several other start-up businesses, such as Apple, had already established solid market positions. In order to get a product on the shelves quickly, the IBM project managers decided to buy the necessary parts, including software, from other companies. This was a new strategy for a company that had always designed, engineered, and built its own products.

Time was not the only factor behind IBM's decision to go with this open architecture strategy for building its personal computer. They also thought that if their machine could be easily upgraded with such things as more memory or larger disk drives, without IBM engineers having to do all the work, it would have a wider market appeal.

One of the things IBM needed most was a language for its new computer. BASIC, because of its ease of use, was the obvious choice. Who better to sell them a micro version of BASIC than Microsoft? IBM called Bill Gates that July to request that he meet with the company

Gary Kidall, President of Digital Research, missed a very important meeting with IBM.
(Seattle Post-Intelligencer)

executives to discuss the purchase of his BASIC for the still top-secret IBM microcomputer. Bill agreed to the meeting.

When the executives from IBM, all wearing the company "uniform" of dark blue suits and white starched shirts, arrived the next day, they initially mistook the twenty-four-year-old Bill for an office boy. But when the negotiations began, they quickly realized their mistake. "He was obviously in control," one of the executives present remembered, "he's one of the smartest men I've ever known."

As in all of their negotiations, the IBM executives asked Bill and Paul to sign a non-disclosure agreement at the beginning of the meeting. This meant no one was to discuss what they talked about outside of the room. Bill and Paul both signed.

Then the IBM men told Gates and Allen they wanted BASIC for their microcomputers. After a lengthy discussion the two companies knew they could do business.

There was one problem, however. IBM still did not have an operating system. The operating system is responsible for managing the computer's functions. It performs roughly the same tasks for a computer that a traffic light system does for a city. It regulates the flow of information, making sure it is delivered to the right place at the right time.

At this time one operating system, called CP/M (Control Program for Microcomputers) was the closest thing to an industry standard. When the IBM executives mentioned their search for an operating system, Bill suggested they fly down to Digital Research in Pacific Grove, California, and talk to the owner Gary Kidall, who had developed CP/M. Bill made an appointment for them to meet with Kidall the next day.

What happened when the IBM executives showed up for their appointment with Kidall has become a legend in the software industry. Like most legends, everyone associated with the events of that day tells a slightly different version. One story is that Gary Kidall was out flying his personal plane and the IBM executives, insulted, left before he returned. Another story is that Digital Research refused to sign the non-disclosure agreement. Kidall, in the years since, has hinted that he was not interested in doing business with IBM, which was seen by many of the youth-oriented microcomputer enthusiasts as an example of everything wrong with their industry.

Although the exact events of that day are fuzzy, the results are clear. The IBM executives left Digital Research without reaching an agreement to buy CP/M. They then asked Bill if Microsoft could provide the operating system, as well as BASIC, within a year. A year was an almost impossibly short deadline, but after hours of discussion with Paul and other Microsoft managers, Bill finally said, "Gotta do it." Microsoft agreed to deliver to IBM an operating system, along with BASIC, in one year's time.

Before that could happen, thousands upon thousands of lines of computer code had to be written. Microsofties, as the employees of Microsoft were beginning to be called, involved in this first IBM project remember those days much the way veterans remember a war.

Oddly, considering the importance the operating system would have for Microsoft's future, the work adapting BASIC was more intense than the work on the operating system, even though BASIC was a familiar language. The reason for this is that the problem of the operating system was solved mostly by a stroke of good luck.

Tim Paterson, a computer engineer, worked for a small company called Seattle Computer. Paterson had built a computer that the current CP/M would not run on. Digital Research promised they would soon release a new version of the operating system that would run Paterson's new machine.

However, Digital Research was slow to develop the new system. The frustrated Paterson finally decided to write his own operating system, based closely on CP/M, but adapted to his new computer. Paterson jokingly dubbed his operating system QDOS, for Quick and Dirty Operating System.

Paterson thought of QDOS as a stopgap measure that would allow his computer to operate until the new version of CP/M was released. When Paul Allen, a friend of Paterson's, heard about QDOS, he asked him who owned the rights. Paterson told Paul that Seattle Computer owned the system, because he had developed it while working there. Microsoft entered into negotiations with Seattle Computer to lease QDOS.

Eventually, after much bargaining, Seattle Computer and Microsoft made a deal. Microsoft won the exclusive right to distribute Tim Paterson's operating system to computer manufacturers, and Seattle Computer received highly favorable terms to sell Microsoft BASIC.

During the negotiations, Bill and Paul never told the managers at Seattle Computer that IBM was interested in licensing QDOS. They did not want the small company to go to IBM directly and cut Microsoft out of the deal. In reality, it would have been difficult for Seattle Computer to make the extensive changes necessary to turn QDOS into a system IBM could use on such short notice. But later, when Seattle Computer discovered that IBM wanted the system, they felt cheated. For the first time, grumbling about Bill's tough business practices started to ripple through the computer industry.

When IBM and Microsoft finalized their deal, Bill remained a tough negotiator. He insisted that Microsoft receive a large royalty for both the operating system, now called the Disk Operating System (DOS), BASIC, and any other languages that Microsoft developed for IBM. He also demanded a royalty for every IBM Personal Compuer (PC) that was sold with DOS and BASIC included. Finally—and most importantly—he insisted that the agreement with IBM be non-exclusive, which meant Microsoft could sell the same product to other computer manufacturers.

It was the final part of the agreement that helped to make Microsoft the largest software company in the world. After the release of the IBM PC in August of 1981, a new standard existed. Although many considered the PC inferior to other microcomputers on the market, IBM's massive advertising campaign, including countless television commercials that used a Charlie Chaplin look-alike, quickly made the PC the standard in the industry. This meant that other computer manufacturers without IBM's financial resources decided to build machines that were compatible with the PC, but sold at cheaper prices. In order to do that they needed the DOS operating system, which only Microsoft could provide.

In the next few years, Microsoft signed deals worth millions of dollars and grew at an amazing speed. With rapid growth came problems. Bill suddenly found himself managing a huge corporation in the most competitive and rapidly changing industry of the 1980s. As the years passed and IBM, among others, realized how much of their fate they had put into Bill's hands, they grew frightened and jealous. Later, the company that had given Bill his first big break would become his archenemy.

That split was years away, however. After closing the deal with IBM, and fulfilling the contract by working himself and the other Microsofties until they collapsed, Bill turned his attention to Apple, the company started by Steve Jobs, who was the other boy wonder of the desktop computer industry.

Chapter Eight

Interface War

Bill Gates is a worrywart. People who know him well say that the tendency to worry is one of his most dominant characteristics. Perhaps his legendary drive, work habits, and volatile temper are driven by the constant fear that he and his company might not stay in front of the rapidly changing technology.

In August of 1981, even while Microsoft was entering the new level of growth made possible by the deal with IBM, Bill saw something that worried him.

What Bill saw was a prototype for the new computer being developed by Apple Computer. Apple, especially in the early 1980s, was the most famous and successful of the new start-up computer manufacturers. Born in a garage in Cupertino, California, Apple had taken the market by storm with its second computer, the Apple II. Now Apple was working on a new style of computer called the Macintosh, after Steve Jobs's favorite type of apple.

By 1981, Steve Jobs had become a favorite of the computer press, and the rags-to-riches story of the hip new computer company made him a legend. Tall, dark, and handsome, Jobs looked like a movie star and could talk about the future in a mesmerizing way.

Jobs invited Bill and other Microsoft managers to come for a demonstration of the Macintosh. The meeting was set to discuss the possibiliy of Apple contracting Microsoft to write software for the Mac.

Bill began to change the way he thought about the future of his industry. With built-in graphics capabilities that seemed ahead of its time, the Mac was a much better engineered machine than the IBM PC. But what really caught Bill's attention was the interface. The small computer industry generated terms and phrases that have since become common. One such term was interface, which describes how the computer interacts with the user. In other words, what the user sees on the computer screen could either be intimidating, requiring a grasp of arcane technology, or, to use another expression then coming into vogue, "user friendly." Bill knew the Mac was more user-friendly than the PC.

When a computer operating in DOS was turned on, the user would be presented with a screen prompt that looked like this: C>. From this point, the operator had to either know or look up all the commands necessary to run a software program, copy a disk, or perform any other function.

The Macintosh was much easier to use. The screen was filled with icons, or tiny symbols, which could be

Bill with Andrew Grove, one of the founders of Intel Corporation, the company that designed the processor chips for IBM computers. *(AP/Wide World Photos)*

pointed at with a cursor controlled by a mouse, a small hand-held peripheral that allowed the user to manipulate the cursor without using the keyboard. With one mouse click, the requested software program opened. Or, if necessary, the user could use the mouse to click onto another icon and delete an unnecessary file. There were other improvements, too. File management was controlled by folders that could be opened just like the paper folders they mimicked. The Mac also allowed multitasking, or the running of more than one program at a time. A simple click of the mouse allowed the Mac user to move between applications.

Steve Jobs wanted Microsoft to write software for his new brainchild. Bill was more than happy to oblige. Over the next few years, Microsoft wrote many of the most popular Mac programs. Microsoft was instrumental in keeping the Mac alive, because other software companies were more interested in developing programs for the larger PC market. The experience of writing applications for Apple, such as the word-processing program Word, allowed Microsoft to develop an application software division. Bill had stuck with languages as long as he could. Now, even he had to admit that it was time to alter his original plans.

The state-of-the-art Macintosh became the computer of choice for many people, especially those working in education and desktop publishing. Bill remained most impressed by the Mac interface. He became convinced that the interface, which is called a Graphical User Interface, or GUI, was the future of the desktop computer. As would become clear later, most of the design of the look and feel of the graphical interface was developed in the 1970s in the legendary PARC lab of Xerox. The problem with GUIs, as Xerox had learned, was that it took a huge amount of memory to run graphical software. Bill had not thought the desktop computer powerful enough to run an operating system that used so much memory. Steve Jobs had shown him that it was possible.

Bill's problem was that the IBM PC, and the dozens of PC imitators, were not powerful enough, and also lacked the necessary hardware to employ a GUI. The original PC did not even have a mouse. The Mac was possible because one company designed and built both the hardware and software. Bill was not a hardware person, so the option of building his own computer with a similar interface was not practical. He would have to wait until the available, and affordable, computers that ran DOS could be manufactured with enough memory to allow for a GUI.

It was a frustrating position to be in, and Bill Gates dealt with frustration the way he dealt with most things. He worked even harder. Bill launched a series of projects that he hoped would push Microsoft into the forefront of GUIs for the PC. There were other smart software developers who had similar ideas.

One of the competing visions of the future of the desktop computer that was prevalent in the mid-1980s was the so-called integrated software package. The idea behind integrated software was that instead of having an operating system that allowed the user to switch between programs, there could be one huge program that would include most of the tools used by the average computer user. One package would include a spreadsheet, database, word processor, calculator, and various other tools. The main advocate of this approach was Mitch Kapor, the president of Lotus Development, the maker of Lotus 1-2-3, the best-selling spreadsheet for the PC. Lotus announced two integrated software packages, Symphony and Jazz, for the PC and the Mac. Bill never missed a chance to speak out against integrated software. He insisted that the memory drain would be too great, and that integrated software would be slow and clunky. He was right. Jazz and Symphony were failures.

Another company eager to enter the GUI software market was IBM. Although Big Blue, as the company is sometimes called, had realigned the microcomputer market, management had started to have some regrets about the way it had designed and developed the PC.

The main source of IBM's regrets was the rapid growth of the "IBM clone" market. Because the PC was designed to be open, it was fairly easy for another company to purchase an IBM computer and reverse engineer it. That is, take the computer apart, find out how it worked, and build their own version. By the mid-1980s, the market was flooded with IBM clones that sold for hundreds of dollars less than the real thing. The new computer makers simply purchased DOS from Microsoft. IBM realized too late the mistake it made by not insisting upon an exclusive deal.

As Microsoft grew, and Bill's personal wealth ap-

Paul Allen and Bill Gates began work on Mircrosoft Windows in early 1982. *(Seattle Times)*

proached the one billion dollar mark, many IBM managers decided they should cut their ties to Microsoft. Other IBM managers wanted to continue the relationship, but only in a way that would allow them to control the final outcome. In other words, the giant corporation was confused about how to deal with Bill Gates. This confusion gave Bill an excellent opportunity. He did not fail to take advantage of it to make his company grow.

Microsoft entered into an agreement with IBM to develop a new operating system that would work in conjunction with a GUI. The new software eventually became known as Operating System 2 (OS/2).

IBM, however, was no longer willing to put all of its eggs in the Microsoft basket. While developing OS/2,

IBM also began work on a different GUI they dubbed Presentation Manager. Big Blue was hedging its bet.

IBM's work on Presentation Manager made Bill nervous. If IBM could set the same standard in operating systems, without Microsoft's help, that they had earlier set in hardware, the future of Microsoft was dim. Bill, though, had no intentin of being left behind. He already had programmers working on Microsoft's own version of a GUI, called Windows. Constantly changing, always behind schedule, the Windows project was further hampered by the political necessity of not angering either IBM or Apple, Microsoft's biggest customers. Apple was worried that Windows too closely resembled the Macintosh GUI. IBM demanded that their OS/2 partner not neglect their joint project in order to develop Windows.

During these years, Bill was like a trick rider trying to stay on top of three horses at the same time. He had to keep Apple happy if he was going to continue to develop applications for that market. IBM needed to be soothed because it could, with a couple of decisions, shift the PC market away from Microsoft. At the same time, he was determined that the development of Windows continue.

The biggest obstacle to the development of a multitasking GUI for PCs was the delay in hardware development. Graphics are large, both in terms of the amount of RAM needed to display and manipulate them on the screen and the amount of disk space necessary to store them. The sophisticated hardware needed to make such a graphical system operational was not yet developed. There was a new processor under construction at Intel, however, that was rumored to be powerful enough to make operating a GUI practical.

The corporate struggle over which GUI would eventually dominate the market continued throughout the 1980s. It was a long, nerve-wracking period, during which, at one time or another, each competitor seemed to be at the top of the pile, only to look around one day and discover they were suddenly at the bottom.

One major blow Microsoft suffered in 1982 was the illness and departure of Paul Allen. During a trip to Europe, Paul discovered lumps in his throat. He cut his trip short, hurried home, and entered the hospital. He was diagnosed with Hodgkin's Disease, a form of cancer that strikes the body's lymph nodes. Although the prognosis for his recovery was optimistic, Paul decided that he wanted to be free from the burden of business. He resigned his position at Microsoft but did maintain control of his stock. When Microsoft began selling shares on the open market in 1986, Allen, who by this time had recovered his health, was suddenly a multi-billionaire. Allen eventually severed all ties to the company he helped found, and today owns the Portland Trail Blazers of the National Basketball Association, along with several other investments.

By the mid-1980s, most of the original Microsofties were gone; replaced by the best recruits Bill could find. Many new hires were graduates of the best schools in the country, such as the Massachusetts Institute of Technology (MIT). The employees of the company were divided into product teams. Each team was responsible for a specific product, such as spreadsheets and word processing programs. Bill was everywhere, constantly checking on the progress of each project, offering his advice, and sometimes losing his temper at what he considered substandard work.

The race for a GUI continued. The work on OS/2 was discouraging. IBM believed in work by committee, in drawing up a design plan and sticking to it, no matter how the situation might change. Programmers at Microsoft worked by defining the desired outcome and beginning to try to achieve it. They took care of problems as they occurred. IBM programmers were rewarded for the number of lines of code they wrote. Microsofties were trained to think concisely—to take the time to make sure they had found the most efficient way to give the computer instructions. Over time, the conflict between the OS/2 development partners led to tense meetings.

In the meantime, Microsoft released two early versions of Windows, both of which were largely ignored by the public. Then, in March of 1988, Microsoft announced the next version of Windows, and shortly afterward their old partner Apple filed legal action against them for stealing the Macintosh "look and feel." It began to appear that the next stage of computer software development might be decided in court.

Chapter Nine

Windows

The emergence of a major software market created confusion in the field of copyright protection. In the early years it became clear that lines of code were protected, just like the language in a book. To steal software code and attempt to sell it under a different name was certainly copyright infringement.

What about a program's "look and feel?" Could a company patent or copyright the way their software appeared on the screen, even if the code was different? When Apple filed its lawsuit, they were attempting to set a precedent; that proprietary rights over the graphical user interface extended well beyond the protection previously afforded to computer code.

Bill was incensed that Apple claimed ownership of all GUI designs. He also thought Apple's legal action was the ultimate act of ingratitude, because Microsoft had kept the Mac alive in its early days by rushing out application software. Without the Microsoft software,

Bill said, the Mac would have become another victim of the IBM tidal wave.

Regarding the notion of copyrighting the "look and feel" of the Mac, Bill had a quick retort that later became famous. He said that he and Steve Jobs were like two burglars who had a rich house in their neighborhood. Both of them had broken into the house and stolen what they wanted, and now Apple was suing Gates because they were angry that he got away with the television.

Bill was referring to the fact that most of the features of both the Mac and Windows had first been developed by Xerox, which had never discovered how to make its computer profitable. By 1980, most of Xerox's researchers had left. Apple hired several of them; so did Microsoft. Bill felt that Apple was trying to gain full control over technology that they had no right to claim. He was determined to fight the lawsuit as hard and as long as possible.

Bill had Microsoft's lawyers file a counter suit charging Apple with slander and attempting to illegally hurt his business. He made two predictions about Apple's lawsuit. First, he was confident Microsoft would prevail; and second, that the lawsuit would drag on for a long time. He was right on both counts.

Despite these legal troubles, Microsoft continued developing Windows and working with IBM on OS/2. Also, the company was finally becoming successful in writing application programs for the PC, especially Microsoft Word and Microsoft Excel, a spreadsheet.

During all the seven-day weeks and eighteen-hour

days, Bill did not have much time to develop a social life. For many years, his work was his life. He loved what he was doing and was more successful than he had dreamed possible. As the years passed, however, he became more aware of the fact he did not have a wife or children. His friends and family insisted that he wanted his own family—he just never got around to it.

For several years he dated Ann Winblad, a computer consultant who had made millions running her own company in Chicago. Most people thought Bill was attracted to her because she had as much "bandwidth," their slang term for intelligence, as Bill. She and Bill grew famous for their reading vacations. She would gather all the available books on subjects they were both interested in, such as biotechnology, and they would go to some beautiful resort and consume as much information on the topic as possible.

They seemed like the perfect couple: two intelligent people with mutual interests. However, as the years dragged on, Ann became impatient. She wanted to have a family and Bill did not seem capable of committing to marriage. Finally, they broke up.

Their relationship was likely a victim of Bill's work habits. It was hard to sustain a long-term love affair while living in different parts of the country. Bill was also consumed with trying to stay on top of the software business. He found time to contribute to charitable organizations, especially the United Way, an organization his mother had long been involved with. He also began buying land in an exclusive neighborhood close to his parents' home in order to someday build his dream house.

Back at Microsoft, the work on the GUIs continued. In the autumn of 1989, IBM announced the release of OS/2, complete with Presentation Manager, IBM's answer to the Mac. The software was released at a gala event in New York City.

OS/2 did not take the industry by storm. There were several problems. OS/2 lacked the ability to run printers made by any manufacturers other than IBM. In an industry where another company, namely Hewlett Packard, was setting the standard for laser printers, this was a mistake. IBM's plan was to sell more printers. But consumers decided not to invest in OS/2.

Another problem was the program's size. In order to run OS/2 at its peak efficiency, the computer needed much more memory than was standard. It was the same old problem. To make OS/2 run, the end users would have to make substantial investments in upgrading their equipment.

The debacle of the initial release of OS/2 began a rift that would continue to widen until it became an irrevocable split between Microsoft and IBM. Bill blamed IBM for the problem. In referring to the immense size of the program Bill jokingly said that IBM's motto should be "Building the world's largest airplane." For its part, IBM blamed Microsoft for undermining the project in order to keep Windows viable in the marketplace. The two companies would continue to cooperate for some time, but never again would they work on joint projects. Later, after Windows had won the battle and become the

Bill holds the packaging for Windows 3.1 in April, 1992. *(AP/Wide World Photos)*

GUI of choice for millions of PC users, IBM would begin actively looking for alliances with other firms as a way to rein in Microsoft's growth.

As Bill predicted, the court battle with Apple continued to drag on. Finally, in the spring of 1992, the chief complaints that Apple had listed in its lawsuit were thrown out of court. Although the decision was not totally conclusive, it went against the idea of one company copyrighting the "look and feel" of its software.

By 1990 the lawsuit itself was almost a moot point. After years of trying, and the premature releases of products that received unfavorable reviews from the industry press, Windows 3.0 was released to great success.

Although the program still had some bugs, it was a major improvement over earlier versions. Two changes made the final breakthrough possible. DOS had been upgraded to provide better utilization of a machine's RAM. One of the improvements was the creation of extended memory, which allowed many of its functions to occur in the background, invisible to the user. The second reason for Windows 3.0's success was the development of the more powerful 80386 and 80486 microprocessors. Hardware had finally caught up with software.

Within six months of its release, Windows 3.0 was selling at the rate of 11,000 copies a day as a retail product, and dozens of computer manufacturers were signing up to ship their machines with both DOS and Windows installed.

Microsoft had, at least for the present, won the battle over which GUI would dominate the PC market. It had

Bill accepts the National Medal of Technology Award from President George H.W. Bush in June, 1992. *(AP/Wide World Photos)*

been a hard-fought battle. Bill had done it in a characteristic way—by keeping his hand involved in all the major, potential competitors to his pet project while also continuing development of his own product. It had been a nerve-wracking period, but in the end Bill Gates was where he wanted to be—on top of the hill.

Microsoft continued to improve Windows. Version 3.1, released in April of 1992, fixed many of the problems with 3.0, and added several features. One of these was the ability to move graphics or information from one Windows program to another; another was to link the data from one file to another. The secret to Windows has always been Bill's insistence that device drivers, the parts of programs that run the printer and mouse as well as instruct software to perform large "block functions," should be the core of the program. That way Windows did not have to be as massive as OS/2.

Other companies were soon developing software to run under Windows. As to be expected, Microsoft had an advantage in this area—one that many competitors felt was unfair. They wondered if it was fair, or ethical, for the same company that sold the operating system, (DOS) and the top-selling GUI (Windows), to also develop and sell applications that ran in conjunction with the two systems. What was to stop a Microsoft Windows programmer from tipping off someone working on Excel or Word about upcoming changes months before the information was released to competing companies? Bill publicly claimed that a "separation of church and state" was established within Microsoft that did1 not allow this to happen. But most were skeptical of this claim. Competitors argued that the now-giant company had what amounted to an illegal monopoly on the software market, and they pressured the Federal Trade Commission to begin an investigation.

But Bill did not let the gripes and complaints deter him. The price of Microsoft stock soared. He was thirty-six years old and, apparently, on top of the world.

Chapter Ten

Competition

In the fall of 1994, *Forbes* magazine, in its annual listing of the 400 richest Americans, placed Bill at the top. His personal fortune was estimated at $9.35 billion. Although he had been ranked near the top in previous years, Bill was considered to be the wealthiest in 1994 because of a steep rise in the value of Microsoft stock. Most analysts attributed the higher values to the U.S. Justice Department's statement that it was ending its investigation of the company for attempting to monopolize the software market.

1994 was a big year for Bill. On New Year's Day he married Melinda French. The couple had met when she came to work in the marketing department at Microsoft. Although their engagement had long been rumored, many of the people who make it their life's work to watch what the richest man in America does expressed surprise that he had gone through with the wedding. Many saw Bill's marriage as an indication that he was slowing down his maniacal work schedule. Bill insisted to the contrary that being married was "more efficient," and should leave even more time for work.

But there were indications that Bill's intense focus on software might be straying a little. He expressed an interest in biotechnology, and invested millions of his own money into ICOS, a company dedicated to developing biotech cures for auto-immune diseases. Perhaps most revealingly, he admitted in interviews that business was "easy."

Bill Gates had by this time become a national figure. Business analysts and historians compared him to Henry Ford and John D. Rockefeller, two of America's most successful, and ruthless, industrialists. He received extensive press coverage. Although some of the reporting was positive, a good deal of it was negative. Some competitors in the computer industry, including several who had done business with Bill, publicly called him vicious and greedy. One irritated competitor called him the "Silicon Bully," and another said that the only difference between Bill and the ferocious velociraptor (from the movie *Jurassic Park*) was that the velociraptor did not make you sign a non-disclosure agreement before it ate you.

Bill attempted to improve his reputation in other ways. He bought an original manuscript by Leonardo Da Vinci, at a cost of $74 million, and made plans to put on public exhibit for everyone to have a chance to see. He gave more interviews than any other American tycoon, and kept a regular speaking schedule.

As he aged, Bill's concern about decadence decreased. He built an estate in Medina, a Seattle suburb, consisting of five sprawling buildings along the shore of Lake Washington. The private residence is more than 30,000 square feet in size, with a full-sized pool and movie theater, among other luxurious features.

Before beginning the house, Bill started a company to the purchase "virtual rights" to the world's great art. The idea was to digitize the images, store them on CD-ROM, and sell the images to art lovers. Although the new company had mixed success, the idea was intriguing. Bill planned to make his new home a virtual museum. Most of the rooms had huge, rear-projection screens connected to a database of more than 300,000 images. Each room could be decorated with a digitized reproduction of any of these great masterpieces.

Bill's new home was yet another example of his desire to stay on the cutting edge of technology. Even though he occupied an enviable position in the business world, he was not content to rest on his successes. He once told a friend that from his earliest days in school his attitude had been "I'll show them."

"Success is a lousy teacher," Bill Gates wrote in 1995. "It seduces smart people into thinking they can't lose." The words come from *The Road Ahead,* Bill's first book. Ironically, the book came out as Microsoft appeared to be on the verge of losing its greatest battle, the struggle for dominance of the Internet. Whereas Microsoft's early programs ran on one computer or a small network, the Internet linked millions of computers worldwide.

Bill Gates and Melinda French greet well-wishers after their mid-winter wedding in Hawaii. *(AP/Wide World Photos)*

As the Internet's popularity and profits soared during the 1990s, Bill's rivals and even many of his admirers wondered if he had indeed been seduced by his success. Microsoft seemed like a sleeping giant during the first months of the explosion of interest and speculation in the Internet. Bill did want to develop an online business as a rival to Internet pioneer America Online, but he still saw the Internet as far less profitable than desktop and office applications.

Gates later admitted that the emergence of the Internet caught him by surprise. The man who had been one of the first to realize that the popularity of the personal computer would not be limited to scientists and engineers failed to have the same foresight when it came to the Internet. There were probably personal reasons for this failure. He was a busy, middle-aged man by the mid-1990s, with a family to take up his time and energy and a giant corporation to run. He was no longer in the trenches, hanging out with young, like-minded computer enthusiasts, where the advances he had profited from originated.

A less personal reason Microsoft was slow to see the Internet's potential is rooted in the way the Internet was developed. Even more so than the personal computer, the Internet was born and nurtured for years deep within government and university think tanks and research labs. It was born out of a need to protect military secrets and as an attempt to guarantee that orders would be carried out in case of nuclear attack. A product of the Cold War between the U.S. and the Soviet Union, the Internet entered public consciousness slowly.

There is no one single founder of the Internet. Rather, it came about after a series of theoretical breakthroughs and inventions made with the financial backing of the U.S. Government.

Digital technology, which made the desktop computer possible, also made it easier, faster, and safer to send information through networks. Information could be broken down into 0s and 1s; organized into small sections, or packets; sent across networks, including telephone lines; and reassembled at its destination. This "packet switching" method was developed by a Pentagon-funded corporation and first made available in 1964. Its original purpose was to protect vital military information in case of nuclear attack. Later, the Pentagon decided to develop a computer network to link universities that did national defense research. The new network, Advanced Research Projects Agency Network (ARPANET) went online in 1969, and used the packet switching technology.

When ARPANET was created computers were huge machines that filled entire rooms. There were a confusing number of different types of mainframe computers, computer languages, and network systems, which made it difficult for computers to communicate over ARPANET. In the early 1970s a universal protocol was developed to make networked information compatible across platforms. Soon afterward, ARPANET was split into different systems. The most prominent new network—NSFNET—was supported by the National Science Foundation, which was funded by the U.S. Congress. This financial support encouraged the development of new,

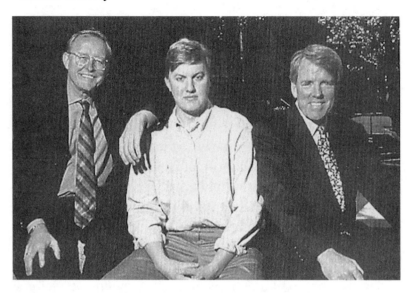

From left: Jim Clark, Marc Andreessen, and Jim Barksdale, the founders of Netscape, the company that presented Microsoft with its first Internet challenge. *(AP/Wide World Photos)*

regional networks. Usually developed and housed at universities and research institutes, these smaller networks were then linked into NSFNET.

After the advent of the personal computer, and the invention of the modem, user groups began sprouting up, creating a loosely linked system of bulletin boards posted on an individual's computer. Access to the Internet, which had become the generic term for the system of interlocking networks, was still difficult for the vast majority of computer users, however. When Microsoft emerged on the scene in the 1980s as the undisputed king of the desktop computer, use of the Internet was mostly limited to professional researchers and computer enthusiasts.

The first step toward making the Internet accessible to

the average computer user was made by the Englishman Tim Berners-Lee. A trained physicist, Berners-Lee worked in a laboratory in Switzerland. He had been intrigued by computers since adolescence, and had built his own computer from components and written software to run on his own machine. When he learned about the American network that had grown up around NSFNET he liked the fact it was not centralized. There was no limit to how large and extensive it could be because it was free to develop without interference. He wanted to find a way to maintain the decentralized structure while also making it available to different computer systems, particularly the desktop computer. He wanted to make the network's complicated structure invisible to the average user.

Berners-Lee's ideal so0lution was to create a uniform system, consisting of a standard language, protocol, and way to assign each computer a specific address. This would link all users into a World Wide Web, the name he assigned to his creation. The new computer language for the Web—Hypertext Markup Language (HTML)—created "hypertext" files that would be recognized by the Web. The new protocol—Hypertext Transfer Protocol (HTTP)—governed how the user moved between files. A Universal Resource Locator (URL) assigned each user an address. After he had created these components, Berners-Lee designed a web site and a crude browser to allow users to move around the web by entering a URL. It was also possible to jump from one site to another by selecting a "hot link." However, this early browser was not capable of displaying graphics.

Word of Berners-Lee's World Wide Web began to spread throughout the computer world in Europe and America. He made no attempt to copyright his creation. His goal was not to market it but to have it spread throughout the Internet as the best method for exchanging information. He even pressed his employer to release the rights to his invention so others could use it and improve upon it.

The World Wide Web began the process of opening the rapidly growing Internet to millions of users. But there were a few more improvements to be made before most people would want to leave their desktop, with the easy to use file system and the colorful GUI interface. As mentioned, Berners-Lee's browser was text only. It was also slow and clumsy and ran only on the Unix operating system, used mostly on corporate networks and mainframes. The world needed a browser that displayed graphics and ran on Windows and Macintosh operating systems.

It is noteworthy that, although the Internet became popular later in the decade of the 1990s as an entertainment and commercial medium, the U.S. government funded its birth and advancement, both directly and through grants awarded to research institutes and universities. This pattern continued even through the development of the first graphical browser, which was the final item necessary to launch the Internet to the general public. It is also interesting that the browser was developed not in the Silicon Valley area of California, which had become linked to the development of software and personal computers, or at the sprawling Microsoft com-

Bill was uncharacteristically slow to realize how quickly the Internet would revolutionize computer use. *(AP/Wide World Photos)*

plex in Redmond, Washington, but at the University of Illinois at Urbana-Champaign.

The University of Illinois sponsored a research facility called the National Center for Supercomputing Applications (NCSA). Supercomputing dealt with more powerful workstation computers that operated off a central server and ran very large, powerful programs. But the younger employees at NCSA, some of whom were also students, knew the days of supercomputers were numbered. One of these students was Marc Andreessen, who became fascinated by the World Wide Web at NCSA. He decided to get a team together to build an improved, graphical browser that ran on the Unix, Windows, and Macintosh platforms. In late 1992, he and a small group of employees of an institute dedicated to developing supercomputers set out to drive a stake in the heart of the supercomputer industry.

They divided into three teams to work on each platform separately. The new Unix browser was finished by January 1993. The other two versions were completed soon after. They dubbed their creation Mosaic.

Mosaic quickly became the most popular browser. But Andreessen and his comrades at NCSA soon realized the fun was over. The academic world did not encourage the type of entrepreneurial behavior they had grown to love. There was also little chance they could profit from their work, since it was done on university time and equipment. After graduation, Andreessen moved to Silicon Valley and soon created a company, along with wealthy veterans of the computer and software industry, to build a new browser. This new company, which eventually was named Netscape Communications Corporation, soon became Microsoft's biggest threat.

Netscape decided to release its browser in a way that would allow it to gain as large a user base as possible. Instead of attempting to sell it at the highest price the market would bear, as Microsoft did with its software, their goal was to become ubiquitous. They decided to only charge a small fee for commercial use. But in reality, there were so many ways to download the browser without paying that few customers ever sent in their thirty-nine dollar fee. Netscape planned to make some money by selling other software and servers, but its ultimate goal was to become the "Windows of the Web" and then to charge customers to add features on to the browser and to collect fees from companies and advertisers. If it worked, this strategy would put Netscape in the same powerful position over the Web that Microsoft held over the personal computer.

Chapter Eleven

Microsoft at War

Netscape's gamble paid off. The thrill of getting a free browser at the click of a mouse helped build excitement about Netscape. More than six million users downloaded the software within a matter of months. When the company went public on the New York Stock Exchange in August of 1995, the new stock soared from $28 a share to more than $58 by the close of its first day of trading. Netscape's founders had turned their upstart enterprise into a $2.2 billion company in one day.

Bill Gates and Microsoft were now in the unfamiliar position of following the technological pack. Bill had considered the Internet browser an application without much profit potential for anyone but operating system vendors. Microsoft executives and programmers had been astonished when America Online paid $30 million for BookLink, an early browser. Even after the market success of Netscape, Bill told a group of Wall Street analysts "An Internet browser is a trivial piece of software."

Netscape's stunning success on the stock market came at an embarrassing time for Microsoft: two weeks before the release of the much-anticipated Windows 95. Bill fumed over the apparent affront.

"They slammed us," Gates said of Netscape's initial public offering (IPO) of its stock, "They used their IPO to do negative PR against Microsoft." The timing was a coincidence, but Netscape employees delighted in having stolen some of Microsoft's glory.

The party for the launch of the new Windows operating system went on, despite the challenge from Netscape. Microsoft worked with software stores to schedule "Midnight Madness" sales. Computer enthusiasts lined up in the middle of the night to be among the first to install the system. The company purchased rights to the Rolling Stones song "Start Me Up" as an advertising jingle. The Empire State Building was lit up in the colors of the Microsoft logo. Champagne flowed at company parties celebrating the release. Bill hammed it up with talk show celebrity Jay Leno at a launch party, joking that Microsoft was so easy to use, even a TV talk show host could do it.

Tucked in Windows 95 was Internet Explorer 1.0. Very primitive compared to Netscape's browser, it was a hastily cobbled together response to the popularity of the Internet. This early version had some interesting features though, including a nice collection of fonts. Even Netscape programmers looked at the product with interest and grudging respect. But after checking out Explorer, they estimated they still had a year's lead-time on Bill Gates's browser, an eon in the fast-moving Internet world.

A glitch in Explorer 1.0 added to Microsoft's troubles with the Internet community. When users with earlier versions of Windows attempted to install it, Explorer caused their previous browsers to malfunction. "In effect your Internet account gets nuked," said Netscape's Andreessen. Actually, the fix was not a difficult one for experienced users, but the bad publicity made its rounds in Internet chat rooms and bulletin boards.

Even worse, the bug fueled suspicions that Microsoft was trying to sell an inferior browser by bundling it with the operating system. Rival companies complained to the U.S. Justice Department, which took the claims seriously. This was the beginning of what would become a long battle between Microsoft and the government.

For the time being, Bill focused on his business competitors rather than the Justice Department. He shifted Microsoft's priorities toward software applications for the Internet. Microsoft's programmers were working far behind the technological curve. In 1995 and 1996, about seventy-five percent of the browser market belonged to Netscape. With Microsoft operating systems running on eighty percent of personal computers in the United States, bundling Explorer seemed the most effective way to beat the competition.

Bill grasped the promise of the Internet, but not the speed at which the technology would develop. At times, he seemed to understand the Internet as clearly as Netscape founders Jim Clark and Marc Andreessen did. In *The Road Ahead*, Bill wrote the next phase of computer development would erase barriers of distance for users.

Bill at the launch of the new version of Windows 95. *(AP/Wide World Photos)*

"The day has almost arrived when you can easily conduct business, study, explore the world and its cultures, call up great entertainment, make friends, go to neighborly markets and show pictures to your relatives, wherever they are—without leaving your desk or your armchair," Bill wrote. "Once this new era is in full swing, you won't leave your network connection behind at the office or in the classroom. Your connection will be more than an appliance you've bought or an object you carry. It will be your passport into a new, 'mediated' way of life."

The media had grown fond of the metaphor "Information Superhighway," filling news stories and broadcast accounts with the term. Bill criticized the comparison to the road system as being outmoded for a breakthrough as big as the Internet. "The highway metaphor isn't quite right, though," he wrote. "It suggests landscape, geography, a distance between points, and it implies that you have to travel, to move from one place to another. But in fact, this new communications technology will eliminate distance. It won't matter whether someone you contact is in the next room or on another continent because this highly mediated network will be unconstrained by miles and kilometers."

Gates suggested that network users would be less like highway drivers than travelers along country roads, with everyone going by various routes to diverging destinations at different speeds. At times, he seemed as visionary as he had in his days as a pioneer programmer.

His main problem was not that he failed to grasp the Internet. He simply miscalculated its quick impact on business, an uncharacteristic blunder for Bill Gates. Even after Microsoft had begun its battle with Netscape and other browsers, at times Bill seemed behind the curve. At a San Francisco press event for the launch of Explorer 4.0 in 1997, he speculated on the future of the Internet in everyday life.

"It's my belief, or my prediction, that a decade from now, the majority of Americans will be living a Web lifestyle," he said. "They will all turn to the Web several times a day for information, entertainment and communication." But, he added, "This is going to take a long time to catch on in a big way." Gates said it would take another decade for the Internet to reach "critical mass," with widespread availability of high-speed connections, flat-panel displays, and PCs that were cheaper than televisions.

Some people in the warehouse audience exchanged surprised glances as Bill continued his speech. Ten years before "critical mass"? Could the leader of the computer revolution actually be saying that it would be 2007 before Americans incorporated the Internet as part of their daily routine? Why, it was happening already. New users arrived on the Internet by the thousands every day. Hardly a day went by without hundreds of stories from the broadcast media and newspapers about the dazzling new technological marvel.

Bill Gates seemed to be stuck in the 1980s, when the use of home PCs grew at a steady, predictable rate. The Internet in the 1990s was not just growing, it was exploding. Brad Silverberg had headed Microsoft's Explorer team. As he listened to Bill's speech from the edge of the stage, he could not quite believe his ears.

"Change, especially change that so directly affects a company's foundations, is hard," Silverberg said later. "Life would have been easier for Microsoft if the world weren't changing so fast."

Life would get even harder—or at least the hours would grow longer—for Microsoft employees. Bill had misjudged the importance of the Internet, but he was not about to accept a position at the back of the pack. The battle for control of the browser market only rekindled his competitive drive. Microsoft still had some of the greatest talent in the industry on its side. It also had its Windows platform, which Bill sought to use as leverage to keep users in the Microsoft world.

Microsoft workers went back to their time-honored strategy of outworking their opponents. Employees who had enjoyed their first long vacations after Microsoft's business victories found themselves back at their terminals as work weeks again stretched to sixty, seventy, and even ninety hours. An internal human resources memo carried the message "The Net is the bet" to 20,000 Microsoft workers.

Netscape was hardly the only threat to Microsoft's empire. Throughout the 1990s, new Internet ideas flew like sparks in a blaze, and many of them posed threats to Microsoft's profits. Linus Torvalds, a twenty-one-year-old computer science student from Finland, created a powerful rival to the Windows operating system when he wrote the Linux operating system in 1991. Torvalds increased the threat by making his source code open, so that other programmers and users could modify it. He also offered it free on the Internet. Windows sold for about one hundred dollars. By the middle of the decade, Linux users boasted that they would bury Windows. Bill and others at Microsoft fretted that a free operating system could indeed ruin the company.

They also worried about Java, a programming language invented by Sun Microsystems. As a language, Java was just one of many innovations that made the World Wide Web more exciting and dynamic. Applications written in Java, for example, could animate previously static images to move like pictures on film. The Java language presented no real threat to Microsoft. The problem came from Java's runtime engine—the code that enabled it to run on Windows computers. Bill stewed over the possibility that Java applications might run better on Windows than Microsoft's own products.

"If you're not taking advantage of Windows [when you run Java], then Windows becomes a commodity," Bill said. "It's ambiguous, because the term Java formally means just the language. But the thing that's often most relevant is the runtime." As with Linux, Java threatened to reduce Windows to irrelevance.

There was not much Bill could do about Linux. Torvalds and his followers were intent on rebelling against the Microsoft establishment. But Bill could work with another corporation. In December 1995, Microsoft licensed Java from Sun. Microsoft company spokespeople claimed that their corporation "loved" the program.

But within the corridors of Microsoft, there was more envy apparent than love. Company programmers worked on a code to replace Sun's language with one that Microsoft could claim as its own. Company meetings and emails stated this hard-hitting competitive goal quite clearly. One project leader sent Gates an email that read, "How do we wrest control of Java away from Sun?" These candid emails would come back to haunt high-level employees and Microsoft.

Meanwhile, the company's applications began to earn some victories with hard-core Internet enthusiasts, particularly Web designers. The goal was still to top Netscape and Sun Microsystems. Microsoft scored a big victory in the Internet battle when it incorporated the use of Cascading Style Sheets into its browser. In July of 1996, twenty-two thousand designers bought out fifty U.S. theatres for a daylong satellite-linked tutorial on the CSS design feature. Prior to Cascading Style Sheets, Web designers had to define the size and look of each element on a page manually. CSS gave designers the ability to create style sheets that automatically set the style for each header and link throughout the document. Web developers were ecstatic at the ease of design. Most importantly, CSS was not a feature supported by Netscape.

Microsoft wanted to prove that it could take on Netscape with products that were just as powerful, adaptable, and cool. But it still used the Windows-Explorer bundling as its front-line weapon in the browser wars. This meant anyone who bought Windows was given a free browser as part of the purchase. Netscape, which had begun to charge a small fee for its browser, was then forced to compete with a free product.

The Justice Department had not forgotten the complaints made by Netscape and other companies that Microsoft had crossed the lines of fair market practice. It is illegal in the United States to operate a monopoly, a business that controls all or almost all of a given market. Attorney General Janet Reno came to believe that Microsoft's bundled software was becoming the cornerstone of a monopoly that already controlled the desktop computer operating system. Microsoft could not be allowed to control the Internet as well.

Microsoft soon found itself in a series of legal wars that would threaten its survival. Sun Microsystems filed suit against the company in October of 1997, alleging a breach of contract of its Java license. The Justice Department filed an antitrust lawsuit against the company in May of 1998, one month before the scheduled release of Windows 98. The suit sought to prevent Microsoft from bundling the Explorer browser with the new version. Joel Klein, who headed the Justice Department's anti-trust division, called Microsoft's bundling policy "an abuse of monopoly power."

The government offered Bill two choices. Microsoft could split its Windows and Explorer units into two separate companies, or it could offer Netscape as part of Windows, a suggestion that infuriated Gates. "It's like ordering Ford to sell autos fitted with Chrysler engines," he wrote in a *Wall Street Journal* opinion piece. "Not only would these proposals undermine our ability to compete, they run counter to the way every industry has evolved over the years—and, more importantly, to what consumers expect when they buy products."

It was easy for Bill to get national exposure to defend himself, but it was another thing to get people to agree wih him. As the world's wealthiest man he was envied by many. And1 his fierce business practices had made him plenty of enemies.

Gates had already begun to give away a good bit of his fortune. He and his wife Melinda set up the Gates Learning Foundation, which gave public libraries greater access to technological resources, and the William H. Gates Foundation, which sought to improve global health. The world began to hear more about his and Melinda's commitment to philanthropy.

In the middle of these bitter corporate battles, Bill and Melinda's first child, Jennifer Katherine, was born on April 26, 1996. The couple's son, Rory John Gates, was born on May 23, 1999. For the first time, Bill began to ponder a life away from Microsoft. He even told interviewers that he would like to retire by the age of fifty. Despite occasional glimpses of his private side, however, much of the public still saw him as a relentless competitor. The struggle Microsoft was engaged in with the highly publicized Justice Department case did nothing to erase this perception.

Initially Microsoft fared badly in court. Part of its trouble originated in the very indignation Gates felt at the charges. He was convinced that the government was engaged in a witch hunt against him and his company.

Bill often travels to investigate how his and Melinda's philanthropic foundation is carrying out its mission in the world's poorest regions. *(AP/Wide World Photos)*

His contempt for the proceedings was shared by most of his top executives. Convinced that the entire suit was an injustice, company executives appeared arrogant in testimony. They also underestimated the evidence against them.

The Justice Department used email from Bill and other executives to reveal how Microsoft bullied both its partners and rivals. A taped deposition showed Bill appearing evasive, attempting to give the impression he had not been involved in major company decisions. Anyone who knew Bill Gates knew this could not be the case. It contradicted the very image of the hard-charging, hands-on manager he had worked to create. Toward the end of the trial, most observers agreed that the Justice Department attorneys were clobbering Microsoft.

In November of 1998, America Online announced a decision that initially delighted Microsoft executives and attorneys. AOL was buying Netscape for $4.2 billion. Microsoft lawyers argued that if two of their most powerful rivals could combine forces to compete against them, how could Microsoft be a monopoly? But the government's lawyers did not buy that argument. They claimed that Microsoft's power over the market had forced Netscape to sell in an attempt to remain competitive. Microsoft attorneys felt that defeat was inevitable.

The verdict came on November 5, 1999. Judge Thomas Penfield Jackson, U.S. District Judge for the District of Columbia, declared that Microsoft was a monopoly. The decision required that Microsoft be split into two companies, one for Windows, the other for Explorer.

Microsoft filed an immediate appeal. Bill was outraged. "This ruling turns on its head the reality that consumers know—that our software has helped make PCs more accessible and affordable to millions," he said. But in matters of business law, courts determine the reality. For the time being, Judge Jackson had turned Microsoft on its head.

Chapter Twelve

Into the Future

The Justice Department's long shadow stretched over Microsoft in the early months of 2000. Since Judge Jackson had ruled the company was a monopoly, Bill Gates' attorneys were struggling to find a way to satisfy the Justice Department that did not involve breaking up the corporation.

In the midst of his company's fight to stay intact, Bill made what seemed a puzzling decision. In January, he resigned as CEO, and gave the job to Steve Ballmer, his former classmate from Harvard. Bill would continue in the office of chairman, and devote his time to software development. He rejected media speculation that the court battles had worn him down and pushed him to the sidelines. Bill said he simply wanted to concentrate on creating new technologies.

He also wanted to carry out some missions that had nothing to do with making a profit. The same month he stepped down as CEO, he and Melinda merged their charitable foundations. The William H. Gates Foundation, which sought to improve global health care, joined with the Gates Learning Foundation, created to provide public libraries access to technology. The new organization was called the Bill & Melinda Gates Foundation. With an endowment of $25 billion, the new foundation set about to improve access to health care and education in developing countries. He and Melinda continued to contribute money to further the foundation's mission. By 2004, the Gates Foundation had committed over $3.2 billion for global health; $2 billion for improved learning opportunities, including Internet access for low-income U.S. communities; and $477 million for community projects in the Pacific Northwest. It also contributed over $70 million to build schools in New York City.

Some people have looked skeptically at this charity work. The Gates Foundation ran into criticism when it gave $25 million to research the genetic modification of food, specifically enriching the vitamin and protein of crops intended to feed the poor. Farmers' groups and social activists claimed that such research would do nothing to address the root cause of hunger, which they said was poverty. They charged that the effort was a Trojan horse seeking to expand biotech research under the guise of good works, and speculated that Microsoft would profit from genetically altered food. Bill denied the claims, saying that poor people's immediate need for vitamins and nutrients outweighed any other consideration.

Bill often said that his personal goals were no longer

just about making money. He pledged to give away ninety-eight percent of his wealth. In his frequent interviews, he talked more often than he had previously about his wife and children. In 2002, a third child, daughter Phoebe, was born. He continued his writing. His book, *Business @ the Speed of Thought*, was published in 1999. In it he wrote that, in the future, networking would become so fast that businesses would have to compete "intuitively." The book became a bestseller.

In June of 2000, Judge Jackson handed down the ruling Microsoft had steeled itself to accept. He ordered the company broken up. Microsoft attorneys filed another immediate appeal.

A year after Judge Jackson handed down his ruling, the legal tide turned in Microsoft's favor. In June of 2001, a federal appeals court overturned Jackson's ruling. Another victory came in the appointment of a new judge in the case. Microsoft attorneys felt that Jackson had shared the Justice Department's skeptical view of the company from early on in the trial, and were glad to see Judge Colleen Kollar-Kotelly replace him.

Microsoft got another boost from a political change. When President George W. Bush took office, his spokespeople signaled that Bush would take a more lenient stand on Microsoft's case than had the administration of President Bill Clinton. In September of 2001, the Justice Department announced that it had no intention of forcing a Microsoft breakup.

Microsoft's tug of war with Sun Microsystems also continued through the courts. In June of 2003, a federal appeals court overturned a ruling that would have forced Microsoft to put Java software on both Windows and Explorer. But it also upheld an injunction prohibiting Microsoft from distributing its own version of Java.

Months after the Justice Department dropped its case against Microsoft, the company unveiled a new gaming technology. The Xbox was billed as the first online gaming device dedicated to fast-action broadband competition. Xbox Live allowed players to play with anyone online. Gamers could also keep a friends list, helping them find their favorite rivals. Xbox Communicator allowed opponents to talk to one another while playing.

The company continued its aggressive development of Windows. Microsoft merged its Windows business and home lines with the release of Windows XP in 2001. The "XP" stood for "experience," meant to summon the image of exciting experiences for PC users. It allowed home users to use instant messaging, play music, and share photos with friends and family more easily. For businesses, XP offered greater speed.

On October 27, 2003, Bill unveiled the most dramatic upgrade since Windows 95 at Microsoft's Professional Developers Conference in Los Angeles. The new product was an operating system code-named Longhorn. The beta version would be available the following year, but it would not premier on the market until 2006.

Microsoft billed Longhorn as both a security fortress and an easier file searcher. Confidential files would go behind an isolated shield within the machine. Users could find their own files with near-perfect ease. They could search the entire hard drive by a variety of methods. The goal was to do away with the file and folder system forever. The side of the screen offered a quick index to the user's favorite activities, such as instant-messenger buddy lists, favorite web sites, or other downloaded information that anyone wanted to display. Graphics reached a new level of sophistication, with windows that turned transparent when pushed aside.

While continuing to fight for dominance in operating systems, Bill mended fences with some of his fiercest rivals. Microsoft partnered with IBM to develop tools that permit computers to conduct secure transactions no matter what platforms they are running, including Windows, IBM's WebSphere, or even the open-source Linux that had cost Microsoft programmers so much sleep.

In September of 2003, Gates went to a technical briefing in Manhattan, where Microsoft and software rival IBM Corporation touted so-called Web services—software aimed at streamlining Internet transactions. To the amusement of reporters, the chairman of Microsoft calmly watched a demonstration of a Netscape browser running on a Linux platform.

"We're being as inclusive as we can," Gates said afterwards. "This is a fabric for someone to do e-commerce that's independent of the operating systems that are out there."

Bill said that Microsoft's work toward the new Web standards would be "royalty-free." Some in the audience could not quite believe they had heard him correctly and questioned Gates about whether he had meant his com-

Bill Gates is determined to help drive technological change well into the twenty-first century. *(A/P Wide World Photos)*

pany would work for no profit. Gates acted as though he could not believe it either. "I can't believe I said that," he joked.

Bill Gates is convinced he and his company have the best understanding of how software-driven technology will develop in the future. He rejects the argument that all the major breakthroughs have been made and that the next decades will be a period of incorporating the improvements of the past into our lives and businesses.

One immediate oncern is the increasing need to protect networks and the Internet from viruses and possible attack. The building of more durable and user-friendly firewalls to protect networks is one project Microsoft is pursuing. Another project is to make email systems that will be better able to separate spam, or junk, mail from other, more necessary, communications.

In the larger picture, Gates plans to use his new position as the top thinker at Microsoft to revolutionize how users interact with computers and other devices running software. One of his long-term desires has been to break down the wall between computers and other electronic devices, such as televisions. Future versions of Windows promise to replace the file and folder system of storing information with an organizational pattern he says will be more intuitive. This new plan is partly a response to the changes that have taken place in the type of information that is increasingly being stored on computers. Now that so much of the data consists of images and sound files, instead of the text files of the past, he thinks there needs to be a better way to move among these type of files. The file and folder method, which requires the user to open a series of individual files and click between them, is a remnant of the paper-based way of working that pre-dated computers and the Internet. Gates feels that the folder system has less relevance to the more graphic-intensive, networked world of information sharing we use today, and he is committed to changing it in future versions of Windows.

Gates sees a bright future for Microsoft and for the development of technology. He credits technological development as being the principal cause of the overall improvement in the U.S. economy that has occurred since the inflation and stagnation of the 1970s, when Microsoft was first incorporated. Over the course of Microsoft's existence, Bill has gone from thinking that the U.S. economy simply benefits from new inventions, to becoming convinced that the development and implementation of new technology is the foundation of America's economy. Contrary to the economic atmosphere that characterized the beginning of his working life, the U.S. and a great deal of the rest of the world are no longer manufacturing-based economies. Because of this fundamental change, it is not possible to think that the major breakthroughs are in the past—not if we want the standard of living in America and the world to continue to improve. Gates is determined that Microsoft will continue leading that development, which he thinks the world is dependent upon, for decades to come.

Bill has given away much of his money since becoming the world's wealthiest man. In this respect, he follows an American tradition. He has been compared to the business tycoons of the early twentieth century, who often became generous philanthropists. Like John D. Rockefeller, who founded Standard Oil in 1870, Gates' business success has brought both criticism and praise.

When historians pass their verdict on Bill Gates, they will have to weigh his best traits against his worst. Will they write that he was an obsessed businessman who used every tool at his disposal to destroy his competitors? Or will they decide he did more good than bad, using the profits of his genius to improve the world?

Gates is not apt to wait passively for answers. As he has done throughout the computer revolution, Bill Gates hopes to continue shaping history with each new technological advance.

Timeline

1955   William Henry Gates III born in Seattle,
        Washington, October 28.
1962   Bill begins public school.
1967   Bill begins attending Lakeside Preparatory School.
1968   Lakeside begins providing students computer
        access.
1971   Lakeside Programmers Group is formed. Bill and
        Paul Allen form Traf-O-Data.
1973   Bill works for TRW.
        Graduates from Lakeside and begins attending
        Harvard University.
1975   Popular Electronics magazine announces the
        release of the Altair 8800. Bill writes BASIC for
        the Altair.
        Microsoft formed in August.
1976   Microsoft begins selling BASIC to the major
        computer manufacturers.
1977   Microsoft wins lawsuit against Pertac.
1979   Microsoft moves to Bellevue, Washington.
1980   Microsoft agrees to develop BASIC and an
        operating system (DOS) for IBM.

1981   IBM PC is released, with DOS 1.0.
        Bill first sees the Macintosh.

1982   Paul Allen leaves Microsoft because of illness.

1983   Time magazine anoints the microcomputer as
        "The Machine of the Year."

1984   Apple Computer releases the Macintosh.
        Microsoft sales reach the $100 million mark.

1985   Windows 1.03 is released to unfavorable reviews.

1986   Bill becomes the world's youngest billionaire.

1987   Microsoft and IBM begin work on OS/2.

1988   Apple Computer files a lawsuit against Microsoft
        over Windows.

1990   Microsoft releases Windows 3.0 to great success.

1993   Windows 3.1 is released.

1994   Bill marries Melinda French on New Year's day.
        Forbes magazine selects Bill as the wealthiest
        individual in the United States.

1995   Microsoft announces the Microsoft Network (MSN).
        Windows 95 is released with Internet Explorer 1.0.

1996   *The Road Ahead* is published.
        Jennifer Katherine Gates is born on April 26.

1997   Explorer 4.0 is launched.
        Sun Microsystems files a breach of contract suit
        against Microsoft.

1998   The Justice Department files an antitrust lawsuit
        against Micrsoft.
        Windows 98 is released.
        America Online buys Netscape for $4.2 billion.

1999   Rory John Gates is born on May 23.
        Microsoft is declared a monopoly on November 5.
        *Business @ the Speed of Though*t is published.

2000   Bill resigns as CEO of Microsoft.
        The Bill & Melinda Gates Foundation is formed.
        Microsoft is ordered to break up.

2001   The order is overturned in appeals court and the Justice
        Department announces it will not pursue a break up.
        Windows XP is released.
2002   Phoebe Adele Gates is born on September 17.
2003   Longhorn is introduced.

Glossary

applications Software designed to perform specific tasks, such as word processing.

BASIC *(B*eginner's *A*ll-purpose *S*ymbolic *I*nstruction *C*ode) An easy-to-learn, high-level programming language.

bit The smallest unit of information that a computer can store.

byte Equals eight bits, or one character.

DOS *(D*isk *O*perating *S*ystem) Provides basic instruction to the computer.

GUI *(G*raphical *U*ser *I*nterface) A user-friendl y display of text and graphics that allows a computer user to interact easily with the computer, typically by using a mouse to make choices from menus or groups of icons.

hacker An expert at programming and solving problems with a computer; also, a person who illegally gains access to and sometimes tampers with information in a computer system.

HTTP *(H*yper*T*ext *T*ransfer *P*rotocol) Defines a set of standards for transmitting Web pages across the internet.

IPO *(I*nitial *P*ublic *O*ffering) The first time stock shares in a company that is going from having limited, private owners to being traded on a stock exchange are offered to the public.

legalese The complicated technical lanuage of legal documents.

mainframe computer The largest, most powerful general-purpose computer systems, designed to meet the computing needs of a large organization by serving hundreds of computer terminals at the same time.

microprocessor The central processing unit in a computer. The microprocessor directs the computer's opertions by use of electrical impulses.

multitasking Performing one or more computer operations simultaneously.

RAM *R*andom *A*ccess *M*emory. Refers to the computer memory used to store information while the computer is turned on.

ROM *R*ead *O*nly *M*emory. Refers to memory that a computer can read but the user cannot manipulate.

URL *U*nivesal *R*esource *L*ocator. An address assigned to each computer connected to the World Wide Web.

World Wide Web The name given to the uniform system designed to organize how users connected and shared information on the Internet.

Bibliography

Auletta, Ken. *World War 3.0: Microsoft Vs. the U.S. Government, and the Battle to Rule the Digital Age* (New York: Broadway, 2002).

Bank, David. *Breaking Windows: How Bill Gates Fumbled the Future of Microsoft* (New York: Free Press, 2001).

Chernow, Ron. *Titan: The Life of John D. Rockefeller, Sr.* (New York: Random House, 1998).

Freiberger, Paul and Michael Swaine. *Fire In The Valley: The Making of the Personal Computer* (Berkeley, CA: Osborne/McGraw-Hill, 1984).

Gates, Bill. *Business @ the Speed of Thought : Using a Digital Nervous System* (New York: Warner Books, 1999).

_____. *The Road Ahead* (New York: Viking Press, 1995).

Ichbiah, Daniel and Susan L. Knepper. *The Making of Microsoft: How Bill Gates and His Team Created the World's Most Successful Software Company* (Rocklin, CA: Prima Publishing, 1991).

Jackson, Tim. *Inside Intel: Andy Grove and the Rise of the World's Most Powerful Chip Company* (New York: Dutton, 1997).

Kawasaki, Gary. *The Macintosh Way* (New York: HarperPerennial, 1990).

Levy, Steven. *Hackers: Heroes of the Computer Revolution* (New York: Doubleday & Co., Inc, 1984).

Manes, Stephen and Paul Andrews. *Gates: How Microsoft's Mogul Reinvented an Industry—And Made Himself The Richest Man in America* (New York: Simon & Schuster, 1994).

Reid, Robert H. *Architects of the Web: 1,000 Days that Built the Future of Business* (New York: John Wiley & Sons, 1997)

Rifkin, Glenn and George Harrar. *The Ultimate Entrepreneur: The Story of Ken Olsen and Digital Equipment Corporation* (Chicago: Contemporary Books, 1988).

Rose, Frank. *West of Eden: The End of Innocence at Apple Computer* (New York: Penguin Books, 1989).

Smith, Douglas K. and Robert C. Alexander. *Fumbling the Future: How Xerox Invented, Then Ignored, the First Personal Computer* (New York: William Morrow, 1988).

Wallace, James and Jim Erickson. *Hard Drive: Bill Gates and the Making of the Microsoft Empire* (New York: John Wiley & Sons, Inc., 1992).

Wallace, James. *Overdrive: Bill Gates and the Race to Control Cyberspace* (New York: John Wiley & Sons, 1997).

Watson, Thomas Jr. *Father, Son, & Co.: My Life at IBM and Beyond* (New York: Bantam Books, 1990).

Index

4004 microprocessor, 31
8008 microprocessor, 30-33, 40
8080 microprocessor, 40, 42,
    50, 52, 54
80386 microprocessor, 80
80486 microprocessor, 80

Advanced Research Projects
    Agency Network
    (ARPANET), 89
Allen, Paul, *19,* 21, 24, 26-27,
    29-33, 35, 38, 40-44, 47,
    48-49, 54, 56, 60-63, *71,* 73
Altair 8800, 39-44, 46, 52, 56
America Online, 88, 96, 108
Andreessen, Marc, *90,* 94, 98
Apple Computer, 51, 58, 64, 65,
    72, 74, 75-76, 80

Ballmer, Steve, 110
Barksdale, Jim, *90*
BASIC, 21, 24, 31, 40, 42-46,
    48-52, 54, 58, 60-63

Berners-Lee, Tim, 91-92
Bill & Melinda Gates Founda-
    tion, 111
Bush, George H. W., *81*
Bush, George W., 112
*Business @ the Speed of
    Thought,* 112

Clark, Jim, *90,* 98
Clinton, Bill, 112
COBOL, 27, 51, 56
Commodore International, 51-
    52, 54
Computer Center Corporation
    (C-cubed), 21-22, 24, 26
Control Program for Microcom-
    puters (CP/M), 60-62

Digital Equipment Corporation,
    20, 22, 56
Digital Research, 59-62
Disk Operating System (DOS),
    63-64, 66, 69-70, 80, 82

Evans, Kent, 18, 21, 24, 26-28, 29

Federal Trade Commission, 83
First Annual World Altair Computer Convention, 50
Forbes, 84
Fulghum, Robert, 29

Gates, Adelle, 9
Gates, Bill, *8, 19, 23, 67, 71, 79, 81, 87, 93, 99, 107, 115*
    antitrust lawsuit, 105-106, 108-109, 110
    Apple lawsuit, 74, 75-76
    bundling, 50, 105
    college, 35-38
    drops out of college, 46-47
    first computer, 20-21
    Lakeside School, 16, 17-25, 26, 28-29, 31, 34-35, 49
    marriage, 84
Gates, Bill Jr., 10, 16
Gates, Jennifer Katherine, 106
Gates, Kristanne, 12
Gates Learning Foundation, 106, 111
Gates, Libby, 12
Gates, Mary Maxwell, 12, 16, 46-47
Gates, Melinda French, 84, *87*, 106, 110, 111
Gates, Phoebe, 112
Gates, Rory John, 106
General Electric, 13, 52

Graphical User Interface (GUI), 68-74, 75, 78, 80, 82, 92
Grove, Andrew, *67*

Harvard University, 22, 35, 44-46, 49, 110
Hewlett Packard, 78
Hypertext Markup Language (HTML), 91
Hypertext Transfer Protocol (HTTP), 91

International Business Machines (IBM), 13, 18, 20, 44, 58-61, 65-66, 67, 69, 70-72, 76, 78, 80, 114
Intel, 30-31, 67

Jackson, Judge Thomas Penfield, 108-109, 110, 112
Java, 103-105, 112
Jobs, Steve, 51, *53,* 64, 65-66, 68-69, 76

Kapor, Mitch, 70
Kidall, Gary, *59,* 60-61
Kollar-Kotelly, Judge Colleen, 112

Linux, 102-103, 114
Longhorn, 113
Lotus Development, 70

Macintosh, *53,* 65-66, 68-69, 74, 75-76, 78, 92, 94

Massachusetts Institute of Technology (MIT), 73-74
Micro Instrumentation and Telemetry Systems (MITS), 39, 41-46, 48-52, 54
Microsoft, 48-52, 54, 55, 57-58, 61-64, 65-66, 68-74, 75-76, 80, 82-83, 84, 86, 88, 90, 94-95, 96-98, 101-106, 108-109, 111-114, 116-117

NASA, 13
National Center for Supercomputing Applications (NCSA), 94
Netscape Communications Corporation, 95, 96-98, 102, 104-105, 108
National Science Foundation Network (NSFNET), 89-91

Operating System 2 (OS/2), 71-72, 74, 76, 78, 82

Paterson, Tim, 62
Personal Electronic Transactor (PET), 51-52
Pertac Computer Corporation, 52, 54
Popular Electronics, 39, 40
Radio Shack, 54
Random Access Memory (RAM), 44, 57, 72, 80
Read Only Memory (ROM), 51, 54, 57

Reno, Janet, 105
Road Ahead, The 86, 98
Roberts, Ed, 39, *41*, 41-44
Rockefeller, John D., 9-10, *11*, 85, 118

Seattle Computer, 62-63
Sun Microsystems, 103-105, 112

Time, 56
Torvalds, Linus, 102-103
Traf-O-Data, 30-32, 37, 40
TRW, 35, 37

Universal Resource Locator (URL), 91
University of Illinois at Urbana-Champaign, 94
Unix, 92, 94
U.S. Justice Department, 98, 105-106, 108, 110, 112-113

Washington State University, 26, 30
William H. Gates Foundation, 106, 111
Winblad, Ann, 77
Windows, 72, 74, 78-80, 82, 92, 94-95, 103-105, 113, 116-117
Wozniak, Steve, 51

Xerox, 56, 69, 76